THE RANDOM HOUSE ACHIEVEMENT PROGRAM IN LITERATURE

READING AND LITERATURE CONSULTANTS

TOM WOLPERT • LEE BENNETT HOPKINS

REVIEWERS

MEI-LING SHIROISHI • **JACKIE MATTHEWS**

Library-Media Specialist   *Curriculum Supervisor*
Chehalem Elementary School   *Hillsborough County Schools*
Beaverton, Oregon   *Tampa, Florida*

Project Editor: Michael A. Ross
Senior Manufacturing Associate: Catherine Bokman
Design and Production: Dimensions and Directions, Ltd.
Composition: Grafacon, Inc.
Cover Photo: Richard Steedman, The Stock Market
Photo Research: Helena Frost and Tracey St. Auburn

ART AND PHOTO CREDIT LIST:

2, George Ulrich; **5, 11, 18,** Meryl Henderson; **23, 24,** Helena Frost / Frost Publishing Group, Ltd.; **26,** Marion Krupp; **28,** Meryl Henderson; **30, 35,** Simon Galkin; **38,** Meryl Henderson; **40, 44, 51, 54, 63,** Hal Frenck; **57,** New York Convention and Visitors Bureau; **68, 71,** Morissa Lipstein; **75,** Alex Bloch; **81,** Fred Tilly, Photo Researchers; **83, 89, 91,** Hal Frenck; **94,** Frost Publishing Group, Ltd; **102,** Richard Steedman, The Stock Market; **96, 107, 112,** MOMA / Film Stills Library; **117, 118,** Simon Galkin; **124,** Frost Publishing Group, Ltd; **125,** Halley Ganges; **127,** Morissa Lipstein; **133, 138,** Mou-sien Tseng; **142,** Library of Congress; **147,** Dick Smolinski; **151, 155,** Kim Mulkey; **158, 160,** Sal Murdocca; **165, 167, 171,** Simon Galkin; **172,** Sal Murdocca; **178, 182,** Morissa Lipstein; **188, 191,** Sal Murdocca; **194, 198, 200,** Meryl Henderson; **202,** Mary M. Thatcher, Photo Researchers; **203, 205, 207,** Morissa Lipstein; **210,** Sal Murdocca; **212, 216, 221, 225,** US Fish and Wildlife Service; **227,** US Forest Service; **234,** US Fish and Wildlife Service; **239,** Karl W. Kenyon, Photo Researchers; **275, 279,** Marion Krupp; **280,** UPI.

Manufactured in the United States of America   ISBN 676-39730-1   6789HL5432

ACKNOWLEDGMENTS

Grateful acknowledgment is made to the following authors, agents and publishers for permission to use copyrighted material:

Atheneum Publishers for "Jennifer", E. L. Konigsberg, excerpted from JENNIFER, HECATE, MACBETH, WILLIAM MCKINLEY, AND ME, ELIZABETH. Copyright © 1967 by E. L. Konigsberg. Reprinted with the permission of Atheneum Publishers, Inc.

Brandt & Brandt Literary Agents, Inc. for "Wilbur Wright and Orville Wright" by Rosemary and Stephen Vincent Benét. From A BOOK OF AMERICANS. Holt, Rinehart and Winston, Inc. Copyright, 1933 by Rosemary and Stephen Vincent Benét. Copyright renewed © 1961 by Rosemary Carr Benét. Reprinted by permission of Brandt & Brandt Literary Agents, Inc.

Curtis Brown Ltd. for "Lassie Come-Home". Reprinted by permission of Curtis Brown Ltd. Copyright, 1940 by Jere Knight. Copyright renewed © 1968 by Jere Knight, Betty Noyes Knight, Winifred Knight Mewborn, and Jennie K. Moore. First published as a short story in THE SATURDAY EVENING POST, Copyright, 1938, by the Curtis Publishing Company. Copyright renewed © 1966 by Jere Knight. "A Tree Called Moses" reprinted by permission of Curtis Brown Ltd. Copyright © 1966 Laura Nelson Baker.

Richard Curtis for "Zoo 2000". Copyright © 1973 by Richard Curtis. Reprinted by permission of the author.

Julia Fields for "Madness One Monday Evening". From POEMS by Julia Fields. Copyright © 1968 by Julia Fields. Reprinted by permission of the author.

Folkways Records for "Vision of a Past Warrior". "As sung by Peter LaFarge on Folkways Records FA 2532. Used by permission."

Harcourt Brace Jovanovich, Inc. for "Primer Lesson" from SLABS OF THE SUNBURNT WEST by Carl Sandburg. Copyright 1922 by Harcourt Brace Jovanovich, copyright © 1950 by Carl Sandburg. Reprinted by permission of the publisher. "Worms and the Wind" from THE COMPLETE POEMS OF CARL SANDBURG, copyright © 1950 by Carl Sandburg, renewed 1978 by Margaret Sandburg, Helga Sandburg Crile and Janet Sandburg. Reprinted by permission of Harcourt Brace Jovanovich.

Harper & Row, Publishers, Inc.: pp. 99–111 from Chapter 8 of SOUNDER by William H. Armstrong. Text copyright © 1969 by William H. Armstrong. Text of Chapter 1 and specified illustration from page 6 of CHARLOTTE'S WEB by E. B. White, illustrated by Garth Williams. Copyright 1952 by E. B. White. Text copyright © renewed 1980 by E. B. White. Illustrations copyright © renewed 1980 by Garth Williams. Text of "Zlateh the Goat" from ZLATEH THE GOAT AND OTHER STORIES by Isaac Bashevis Singer. Text copyright © 1966 by Isaac Bashevis Singer. Reprinted by permission of the publisher.

William Heinemann Ltd for excerpt from THINGS FALL APART by Chinua Achebe. Reprinted by permission of William Heinemann Ltd.

International Creative Management, Inc. for "Grandpa and the Statue" by Arthur Miller. Reprinted by permission of International Creative Management, Inc. Copyright © 1945, 1973 by Arthur Miller.

Francisco Jiménez for "The Circuit". From ARIZONA QUARTERLY, Autumn 1973. Reprinted by permission of the author and THE ARIZONA QUARTERLY.

Macmillan Publishing Company. Reprinted with permission of Macmillan Publishing Company: From HANDS UP! by Ruth Goode. Text copyright © 1983 by Ruth Goode. From THE LION, THE WITCH AND THE WARDROBE by C. S. Lewis. Copyright 1950 C.S. Lewis Pte. Ltd., copyright renewed 1978. "Swift Things Are Beautiful" from AWAY GOES SALLY by Elizabeth Coatsworth. Copyright 1934 by Macmillan Publishing Company, renewed 1962 by Elizabeth Coatsworth Beston. From ZEELY by Virginia Hamilton. Text copyright © 1967 by Virginia Hamilton.

Eve Merriam for "The Stray Cat" from CATCH A LITTLE RHYME by Eve Merriam. Copyright © 1966 by Eve Merriam. Reprinted by permission of the author.

William Morrow and Company, Inc. for Chapter 3 in THE ADVENTURES OF PINOCCHIO by C. Collodi. Translated by M. L. Rosenthal. By permission of Lothrop, Lee and Shepard Books (A Division of William Morrow and Company).

TABLE OF CONTENTS

LAUGHTER IS THE BEST MEDICINE.

Father William	*Lewis Carroll*	2
All Things Wise and Wonderful (excerpt)	*James Herriot*	4
Riddle	*Ian Serraillier*	23
Who Am I?	*Felice Holman*	24
The Scotty Who Knew Too Much	*James Thurber*	25
The Dog That Talked	*Traditional*	28
Sounder (excerpt)	*William H. Armstrong*	29

IT MATTERS NOT HOW LONG WE LIVE, BUT HOW.

I May Be Silent, But	*Tsuboi Shigeji*	38
Zeely (excerpt)	*Virginia Hamilton*	39
Grandpa and the Statue	*Arthur Miller*	50
The Spider Plant (excerpt)	*Yetta Speevack*	67
Worms and the Wind	*Carl Sandburg*	75
Charlotte's Web (excerpt)	*E. B. White*	77
Afternoon	*Robert Sund*	81
Raymond's Run	*Toni Cade Bambara*	82
Madness One Monday Evening	*Julia Fields*	94
The Black Stallion (excerpt)	*Walter Farley*	95
The Circuit	*Francisco Jiménez*	116
Primer Lesson	*Carl Sandburg*	124
Vision of a Past Warrior	*Peter La Farge*	125
Thank You, M'am	*Langston Hughes*	126
The Big Wave	*Pearl S. Buck*	132
The Wright Brothers (excerpt)	*Quentin Reynolds*	141
Wilbur Wright and Orville Wright	*Rosemary and Stephen Vincent Benét*	147

IMAGINATION IS THE EYE OF THE SOUL.

Alice — Shel Silverstein — 150
Alice's Adventures in Wonderland (excerpt) — Lewis Carroll — 151
A Strange Sled Race — Vivian Thompson — 158
Jennifer, Hecate, Macbeth, William McKinley, and Me, Elizabeth (excerpt) — E. L. Konigsburg — 163
The Lion, the Witch and the Wardrobe (excerpt) — C. S. Lewis — 172
Things Fall Apart (excerpt) — Chinua Achebe — 177
Zoo 2000 — Richard Curtis — 181
The Adventures of Pinocchio: Tale of a Puppet (excerpt) — C. Collodi — 188
Three Strong Women — Claus Stamm — 193

NATURE AND WISDOM ALWAYS SAY THE SAME.

The Stray Cat — Eve Merriam — 202
Zlateh the Goat — Isaac Bashevis Singer — 203
The Tiger Behind the Fox — Chan Kuo Ts'e — 210
Bambi: A Life in the Woods (excerpt) — Felix Salten — 211
A Tree Called Moses — Laura Nelson Baker — 226
Hands Up! (excerpt) — Ruth Goode — 237
Gorilla Gorilla (excerpt) — Carol Fenner — 241
Lassie Come-Home (excerpt) — Eric Knight — 274
Swift Things Are Beautiful — Elizabeth Coatsworth — 280

TO THE STUDENT

We are born into a world that we know nothing about. As we grow, we begin to learn about the immediate world that surrounds us and the world of ideas, experiences, and people that exists beyond our reach. Sometimes we are fortunate to meet a person who can share experiences with us. But what about those ideas and experiences that we cannot touch or hear about? How do we know about the worlds of the past and the dreams of the future? Literature is the answer. Literature opens the door to new worlds.

As you read this book many authors will begin to share their worlds with you. Not only what they say, but how they say it, is important. You will experience new ideas . . . new thoughts. You will find your emotions being excited as you cry or laugh at what others have to share.

The beauty of all this is that all you have to do is read. You don't have to leave your world to discover the excitement of living in new and different places. Between the pages of a book you can discover loneliness and happiness; young life and old life; frustration and inspiration; mystery and intrigue; the real and the make-believe. All of this is yours to explore by reading literature.

Laughter is the best medicine.

Father William

Lewis Carroll

"You are old, Father William," the young man said,
  "And your hair has become very white;
And yet you incessantly stand on your head—
  Do you think, at your age, it is right?"

"In my youth," Father William replied to his son,
  "I feared it might injure the brain;
But, now that I'm perfectly sure I have none,
  Why, I do it again and again."

"You are old," said the youth, "as I mentioned before,
  And have grown most uncommonly fat;
Yet you turned a back-somersault in at the door—
  Pray, what is the reason of that?"

"In my youth," said the sage, as he shook his gray locks,
  "I kept all my limbs very supple
By the use of this ointment—one shilling the box—
  Allow me to sell you a couple?"

"You are old," said the youth, "and your jaws are too weak
  For anything tougher than suet;
Yet you finished the goose, with the bones and the beak—
  Pray, how did you manage to do it?"

"In my youth," said his father, "I took to the law,
  And argued each case with my wife;
And the muscular strength which it gave to my jaw
  Has lasted the rest of my life."

"You are old," said the youth, "one would hardly suppose
  That your eye was as steady as ever;
Yet you balanced an eel on the end of your nose—
  What made you so awfully clever?"

"I have answered three questions, and that is enough,"
  Said his father; "don't give yourself airs!
Do you think I can listen all day to such stuff?
  Be off, or I'll kick you downstairs!"

excerpt from

All Things
Wise and Wonderful

James Herriot

All Things Wise and Wonderful *is just one of several autobiographical books written by James Herriot, a veterinarian living and working in northern England. Each book tells of Herriot's experiences taking care of farm animals and pets (and their owners!) in a rural setting. In* All Things Wise and Wonderful, *Herriot is serving in the Royal Air Force. He tells his stories in flashback. In this selection, he remembers how he and his partner's brother, Tristan, saved a cat's life against all odds. It turned out that the cat had a very unusual "hobby."*

I had plenty of time on my hands at Eastchurch, plenty of time to think, and like most servicemen I thought of home. Only my home wasn't there any more.

When I left Darrowby Helen had gone back to live with her father and the little rooms under the tiles of Skeldale House would be empty and dusty now. But they lived on in my mind, clear in every detail.

I could see the ivy-fringed window looking over the tumble of roofs to the green hills, our few pieces of furniture, the bed and side table and the old wardrobe which only stayed shut with the aid of one of my socks jammed in the door. Strangely, it was that dangling woollen toe which gave me the sharpest stab as I remembered.

And even though it was all gone I could hear the bedside radio playing, my wife's voice from the other side of the fire and on that winter evening Tristan shouting up the stairs from the passage far below.

"Jim! Jim!"

I went out and stuck my head over the bannisters. "What is it, Triss?"

"Sorry to bother you, Jim, but could you come down for a minute?" The upturned face had an anxious look.

I went down the long flights of steps two at a time and when I arrived slightly breathless on the ground floor Tristan beckoned me through to the consulting room at the back of the house. A teenage girl was standing by the table, her hand resting on a stained roll of blanket.

"It's a cat," Tristan said. He pulled back a fold of the blanket and I looked down at a large, deeply striped tabby. At least he would have been large if he had had any flesh on his bones, but ribs and pelvis stood out painfully through the fur and as I passed my hand over the motionless body I could feel only a thin covering of skin.

Tristan cleared his throat. "There's something else, Jim."

I looked at him curiously. For once he didn't seem to have a joke in him. I watched as he gently lifted one of the cat's hind legs and rolled the abdomen into view. There was a gash on the ventral surface through which a coiled cluster of intestines spilled grotesquely on to the cloth. I was still shocked and staring when the girl spoke.

"I saw this cat sittin' in the dark, down Brown's yard. I thought 'e looked skinny, like, and a bit quiet and I bent down to give 'im a pat. Then I saw 'e was badly hurt and I went home for a blanket and brought 'im round to you."

"That was kind of you," I said. "Have you any idea who he belongs to?"

The girl shook her head. "No, he looks like a stray to me."

"He does indeed." I dragged my eyes away from the terrible wound. "You're Marjorie Simpson, aren't you?"

"Yes."

"I know your Dad well. He's our postman."

"That's right." She gave a half smile then her lips trembled.

"Well, I reckon I'd better leave 'im with you. You'll be goin' to put him out of his misery. There's nothing anybody can do about . . . about that?"

I shrugged and shook my head. The girl's eyes filled with tears, she stretched out a hand and touched the emaciated animal then turned and walked quickly to the door.

"Thanks again, Marjorie," I called after the retreating back. "And don't worry—we'll look after him."

In the silence that followed, Tristan and I looked down at the shattered animal. Under the surgery lamp it was all too easy to see. He had almost been disembowelled and the pile of intestines was covered in dirt and mud.

"What d'you think did this?" Tristan said at length. "Has he been run over?"

"Maybe," I replied. "Could be anything. An attack by a big dog or somebody could have kicked him or struck him." All things were possible with cats because some people seemed to regard them as fair game for any cruelty.

Tristan nodded. "Anyway, whatever happened, he must have been on the verge of starvation. He's a skeleton. I bet he's wandered miles from home."

"Ah well," I sighed. "There's only one thing to do. Those guts are perforated in several places. It's hopeless."

Tristan didn't say anything but he whistled under his breath and drew the tip of his forefinger again and again across the furry cheek. And, unbelievably, from somewhere in the scraggy chest a gentle purring arose.

The young man looked at me, round eyed. "My God, do you hear that?"

"Yes . . . amazing in that condition. He's a good natured cat."

Tristan, head bowed, continued his stroking. I knew how he felt because, although he preserved a cheerfully hard-boiled attitude to our patients he couldn't kid me about one thing; he had a soft spot for cats. Even now, when we are both around the sixty mark, he often talks to me over a beer about the cat he has had for many years. It is a typical relationship—they tease each other unmercifully—but it is based on real affection.

"It's no good, Triss," I said gently. "It's got to be done." I reached for the syringe but something in me rebelled against plunging a needle into that mutilated

7

body. Instead I pulled a fold of the blanket over the cat's head.

"Pour a little ether on to the cloth," I said. "He'll just sleep away."

Wordlessly Tristan unscrewed the cap of the ether bottle and poised it above the head. Then from under the shapeless heap of blanket we heard it again; the deep purring which increased in volume till it boomed in our ears like a distant motor cycle.

Tristan was like a man turned to stone, hand gripping the bottle rigidly, eyes staring down at the mound of cloth from which the purring rose in waves of warm friendly sound.

At last he looked up at me and gulped. "I don't fancy this much, Jim. Can't we do something?"

"You mean, put that lot back?"

"Yes."

"But the bowels are damaged—they're like a sieve in parts."

"We could stitch them, couldn't we?"

I lifted the blanket and looked again. "Honestly, Triss, I wouldn't know where to start. And the whole thing is filthy."

He didn't say anything, but continued to look at me steadily. And I didn't need much persuading. I had no more desire to pour ether on to that comradely purring than he had.

"Come on, then," I said. "We'll have a go."

With the oxygen bubbling and the cat's head in the anaesthetic mask we washed the whole prolapse with warm saline. We did it again and again but it was impossible to remove every fragment of caked dirt. Then we started the painfully slow business of stitching the many holes in the tiny intestines, and here I was glad of Tristan's nimble fingers which seemed better able to manipulate the small round-bodied needles than mine.

Two hours and yards of catgut later, we dusted the patched up peritoneal surface with sulphanilamide and pushed the entire mass back into the abdomen. When I had sutured muscle layers and skin everything looked tidy

8

but I had a nasty feeling of sweeping undesirable things under the carpet. The extensive damage, all that contamination—peritonitis was inevitable.

"He's alive, anyway, Triss," I said as we began to wash the instruments. "We'll put him on to sulphapyridine and keep our fingers crossed." There were still no antibiotics at that time but the new drug was a big advance.

The door opened and Helen came in. "You've been a long time, Jim." She walked over to the table and looked down at the sleeping cat. "What a poor skinny little thing. He's all bones."

"You should have seen him when he came in." Tristan switched off the steriliser and screwed shut the valve on the anaesthetic machine. "He looks a lot better now."

She stroked the little animal for a moment. "Is he badly injured?"

"I'm afraid so, Helen," I said. "We've done our best for him but I honestly don't think he has much chance."

"What a shame. And he's pretty, too. Four white feet and all those unusual colours." With her finger she traced the faint bands of auburn and copper-gold among the grey and black.

Tristan laughed. "Yes, I think that chap has a ginger Tom somewhere in his ancestry."

Helen smiled, too, but absently, and I noticed a broody look about her. She hurried out to the stock room and returned with an empty box.

"Yes . . . yes . . ." she said thoughtfully. "I can make a bed in this box for him and he'll sleep in our room, Jim."

"He will?"

"Yes, he must be warm, mustn't he?"

"Of course."

Later, in the darkness of our bed-sitter, I looked from my pillow at a cosy scene. Sam in his basket on one side of the flickering fire and the cat cushioned and blanketed in his box on the other.

As I floated off into sleep it was good to know that my patient was so comfortable, but I wondered if he would be alive in the morning. . . .

I knew he was alive at 7:30 A.M. because my wife was already up and talking to him. I trailed across the room in my pajamas and the cat and I looked at each other. I rubbed him under the chin and he opened his mouth in a rusty miaow. But he didn't try to move.

"Helen," I said. "This little thing is tied together inside with catgut. He'll have to live on fluids for a week and even then he probably won't make it. If he stays up here you'll be spooning milk into him umpteen times a day."

"Okay, okay." She had that broody look again.

It wasn't only milk she spooned into him over the next few days. Beef essence, strained broth and a succession of sophisticated baby foods found their way down his throat at regular intervals. One lunch time I found Helen kneeling by the box.

"We shall call him Oscar," she said.

"You mean we're keeping him?"

"Yes."

I am fond of cats but we already had a dog in our cramped quarters and I could see difficulties. Still I decided to let it go.

"Why Oscar?"

"I don't know." Helen tipped a few drops of chop gravy on to the little red tongue and watched intently as he swallowed.

One of the things I like about women is their mystery, the unfathomable part of them, and I didn't press the matter further. But I was pleased at the way things were going. I had been giving him the sulphapyridine every six hours and taking the temperature night and morning, expecting all the time to encounter the roaring fever, the vomiting and the tense abdomen of peritonitis. But it never happened.

It was as though Oscar's animal instinct told him he had to move as little as possible because he lay absolutely still day after day and looked up at us—and purred.

His purr became part of our lives and when he eventually left his bed, sauntered through to our kitchen and began to sample Sam's dinner of meat and biscuit it was a moment of triumph. And I didn't spoil it by wondering if he was ready for solid food; I felt he knew.

From then on it was sheer joy to watch the furry scarecrow fill out and grow strong, and as he ate and ate and the flesh spread over his bones the true beauty of his coat showed in the glossy medley of auburn, black and gold. We had a handsome cat on our hands.

Once Oscar had fully recovered, Tristan was a regular visitor.

He probably felt, and rightly, that he, more than I, had saved Oscar's life in the first place and he used to play with him for long periods. His favourite ploy was to push his leg round the corner of the table and withdraw it repeatedly just as the cat pawed at it.

Oscar was justifiably irritated by this teasing but showed his character by lying in wait for Tristan one night and biting him smartly in the ankle before he could start his tricks.

From my own point of view Oscar added many things to our menage. Sam was delighted with him and the two soon became firm friends. Helen adored him and each evening I thought afresh that a nice cat washing his face by the hearth gave extra comfort to a room.

Oscar had been established as one of the family for several weeks when I came in from a late call to find Helen waiting for me with a stricken face.

"What's happened?" I asked.

"It's Oscar—he's gone!"

"Gone? What do you mean?"

"Oh, Jim, I think he's run away."

I stared at her. "He wouldn't do that. He often goes down to the garden at night. Are you sure he isn't there?"

"Absolutely. I've searched right into the yard. I've even had a walk round the town. And remember." Her chin quivered. "He . . . he ran away from somewhere before."

I looked at my watch. "Ten o'clock. Yes, that is strange. He shouldn't be out at this time."

As I spoke the front door bell jangled. I galloped down the stairs and as I rounded the corner in the passage I could see Mrs Heslington, the vicar's wife, through the glass. I threw open the door. She was holding Oscar in her arms.

12

"I believe this is your cat, Mr Herriot," she said.

"It is indeed, Mrs Heslington. Where did you find him?"

She smiled. "Well it was rather odd. We were having a meeting of the Mothers' Union at the church house and we noticed the cat sitting there in the room."

"Just sitting . . . ?"

"Yes, as though he were listening to what we were saying and enjoying it all. It was unusual. When the meeting ended I thought I'd better bring him along to you."

"I'm most grateful, Mrs Heslington." I snatched Oscar and tucked him under my arm. "My wife is distraught— she thought he was lost."

It was a little mystery. Why should he suddenly take off like that? But since he showed no change in his manner over the ensuing week we put it out of our minds.

Then one evening a man brought in a dog for a distemper inoculation and left the front door open. When I went up to our flat I found that Oscar had disappeared again. This time Helen and I scoured the market place and side alleys in vain and when we returned at half past nine we were both despondent. It was nearly eleven and we were thinking of bed when the door bell rang.

It was Oscar again, this time resting on the ample stomach of Jack Newbould. Jack was leaning against a doorpost and the fresh country air drifting in from the dark street was richly intermingled with beer fumes.

Jack was a gardener at one of the big houses. He hiccuped gently and gave me a huge benevolent smile. "Brought your cat, Mr Herriot."

"Gosh, thanks, Jack!" I said, scooping up Oscar gratefully. "Where the devil did you find him?"

"Well, s'matter o' fact, 'e sort of found me."

"What do you mean?"

Jack closed his eyes for a few moments before articulating carefully. "Thish is a big night, tha knows, Mr Herriot. Darts championship. Lots of t'lads round at t'Dog and Gun—lotsh and lotsh of 'em. Big gatherin'."

"And our cat was there?"

"Aye, he were there, all right. Sittin' among t'lads. Shpent t'whole evenin' with us."

"Just sat there, eh?"

"That 'e did." Jack giggled reminiscently. "By gaw 'e enjoyed 'isself. Ah gave 'im a drop o' best bitter out of me own glass and once or twice ah thought 'e was goin' to have a go at chuckin' a dart. He's some cat." He laughed again.

As I bore Oscar upstairs I was deep in thought. What was going on here? These sudden desertions were upsetting Helen, and I felt they could get on my nerves in time.

I didn't have long to wait till the next one. Three nights later he was missing again. This time Helen and I didn't bother to search—we just waited.

He was back earlier than usual. I heard the door bell at nine o'clock. It was the elderly Miss Simpson peering through the glass. And she wasn't holding Oscar—he was prowling on the mat waiting to come in.

Miss Simpson watched with interest as the cat stalked inside and made for the stairs. "Ah, good, I'm so glad he's come home safely. I knew he was your cat and I've been intrigued by his behaviour all evening."

"Where . . . may I ask?"

"Oh, at the Women's Institute. He came in shortly after we started and stayed there till the end."

"Really? What exactly was your programme, Miss Simpson?"

"Well, there was a bit of committee stuff, then a short talk with lantern slides by Mr Walters from the water company and we finished with a cake-making competition."

"Yes . . . yes . . . and what did Oscar do?"

She laughed. "Mixed with the company, apparently enjoyed the slides and showed great interest in the cakes."

"I see. And you didn't bring him home?"

"No, he made his own way here. As you know, I have to pass your house and I merely rang your bell to make sure you knew he had arrived."

"I'm obliged to you, Miss Simpson. We were a little worried."

I mounted the stairs in record time. Helen was sitting with the cat on her knee and she looked up as I burst in.

"I know about Oscar now," I said.

"Know what?"

"Why he goes on these nightly outings. He's not running away—he's visiting."

"Visiting?"

"Yes," I said. "Don't you see? He likes getting around, he loves people, especially in groups, and he's interested in what they do. He's a natural mixer."

Helen looked down at the attractive mound of fur curled on her lap. "Of course . . . that's it . . . he's a socialite!"

"Exactly, a high stepper!"

"A cat-about-town!"

It all afforded us some innocent laughter and Oscar sat up and looked at us with evident pleasure, adding his own throbbing purr to the merriment. But for Helen and me there was a lot of relief behind it; ever since our cat had started his excursions there had been the gnawing fear that we would lose him, and now we felt secure.

From that night our delight in him increased. There was endless joy in watching this facet of his character unfolding. He did the social round meticulously, taking in most of the activities of the town. He became a familiar figure at whist drives, jumble sales, school concerts and scout bazaars. Most of the time he was made welcome, but was twice ejected from meetings of the Rural District Council who did not seem to relish the idea of a cat sitting in on their deliberations.

At first I was apprehensive about his making his way through the streets but I watched him once or twice and saw that he looked both ways before tripping daintily across. Clearly he had excellent traffic sense and this made me feel that his original injury had not been caused by a car.

Taking it all in all, Helen and I felt that it was a kind stroke of fortune which had brought Oscar to us. He was a warm and cherished part of our home life. He added to our happiness.

When the blow fell it was totally unexpected.

I was finishing the evening surgery. I looked round the door and saw only a man and two little boys.

"Next, please," I said.

The man stood up. He had no animal with him. He was middle-aged, with the rough weathered face of a farm worker. He twirled a cloth cap nervously in his hands.

"Mr Herriot?" he said.

"Yes, what can I do for you?"

He swallowed and looked me straight in the eyes. "Ah think you've got ma cat."

"What?"

"Ah lost ma cat a bit since." He cleared his throat. "We used to live at Missdon but ah got a job as ploughman to Mr Horne of Wederly. It was after we moved to Wederly that t'cat went missin'. Ah reckon he was tryin' to find 'is way back to his old home."

"Wederly? That's on the other side of Brawton—over thirty miles away."

"Aye, ah knaw, but cats is funny things."

"But what makes you think I've got him?"

He twisted the cap around a bit more. "There's a cousin o' mine lives in Darrowby and ah heard tell from 'im about this cat goes around to meetin's. I 'ad to come. We've been huntin' everywhere."

"Tell me," I said. "This cat you lost. What did he look like?"

"Grey and black and sort o' gingery. Right bonny 'e was. And 'e was allus goin' out to gatherin's."

A cold hand clutched at my heart. "You'd better come upstairs. Bring the boys with you."

Helen was putting some coal on the fire of the bed-sitter.

"Helen," I said. "This is Mr—er—I'm sorry, I don't know your name."

"Gibbons, Sep Gibbons. They called me Septimus because ah was the seventh in family and it looks like ah'm goin' t'same way 'cause we've got six already. These are our two youngest." The two boys, obvious twins of about eight, looked up at us solemnly.

I wished my heart would stop hammering. "Mr. Gibbons thinks Oscar is his. He lost his cat some time ago."

My wife put down her little shovel. "Oh . . . oh . . . I see." She stood very still for a moment then smiled faintly. "Do sit down. Oscar's in the kitchen, I'll bring him through."

She went out and reappeared with the cat in her arms. She hadn't got through the door before the little boys gave tongue.

"Tiger!" they cried. "Oh, Tiger, Tiger!"

The man's face seemed lit from within. He walked quickly across the floor and ran his big work-roughened hand along the fur.

"Hullo, awd lad," he said, and turned to me with a radiant smile. "It's 'im, Mr Herriot. It's 'im awright, and don't 'e look well!"

"You call him Tiger, eh?" I said.

"Aye," he replied happily. "It's them gingery stripes. The kids called 'im that. They were broken hearted when we lost 'im."

As the two little boys rolled on the floor our Oscar rolled with them, pawing playfully, purring with delight.

Sep Gibbons sat down again. "That's the way 'e allus went on wi' the family. They used to play with 'im for hours. By gaw we did miss 'im. He were a right favourite."

I looked at the broken nails on the edge of the cap, at the decent, honest, uncomplicated Yorkshire face so like the many I had grown to like and respect. Farm men like him got thirty shillings a week in those days and it was reflected in the threadbare jacket, the cracked, shiny boots and the obvious hand-me-downs of the boys.

But all three were scrubbed and tidy, the man's face like a red beacon, the children's knees gleaming and their hair carefully slicked across their foreheads. They looked like nice people to me. I didn't know what to say.

Helen said it for me. "Well, Mr Gibbons." Her tone had an unnatural brightness. "You'd better take him."

The man hesitated. "Now then, are ye sure, Missis Herriot?"

"Yes . . . yes, I'm sure. He was your cat first."

"Aye, but some folks 'ud say finders keepers or summat like that. Ah didn't come 'ere to demand 'im back or owt of t'sort."

"I know you didn't, Mr. Gibbons, but you've had him all those years and you've searched for him so hard. We couldn't possibly keep him from you."

He nodded quickly. "Well, that's right good of ye." He paused for a moment, his face serious, then he stooped and picked Oscar up. "We'll have to be off if we're goin' to catch the eight o'clock bus."

Helen reached forward, cupped the cat's head in her hands and looked at him steadily for a few seconds. Then she patted the boys' heads. "You'll take good care of him, won't you?"

"Aye, missis, thank ye, we will that." The two small faces looked up at her and smiled.

"I'll see you down the stairs, Mr Gibbons," I said.

On the descent I tickled the furry cheek resting on the man's shoulder and heard for the last time the rich purring. On the front door step we shook hands and they set off down the street. As they rounded the corner of Trengate they stopped and waved, and I waved back at the man, the two children and the cat's head looking back at me over the shoulder.

It was my habit at that time in my life to mount the stairs two or three at a time but on this occasion I trailed upwards like an old man, slightly breathless, throat tight, eyes prickling.

I cursed myself for a sentimental fool but as I reached our door I found a flash of consolation. Helen had taken it remarkably well. She had nursed that cat and grown deeply attached to him, and I'd have thought an unforeseen calamity like this would have upset her terribly. But no, she had behaved calmly and rationally. You never knew with women, but I was thankful.

It was up to me to do as well. I adjusted my features into the semblance of a cheerful smile and marched into the room.

Helen had pulled a chair close to the table and was slumped face down against the wood. One arm cradled her head while the other was stretched in front of her as her body shook with an utterly abandoned weeping.

I had never seen her like this and I was appalled. I tried to say something comforting but nothing stemmed the flow of racking sobs.

Feeling helpless and inadequate I could only sit close to her and stroke the back of her head. Maybe I could have said something if I hadn't felt just about as bad myself.

You get over these things in time. After all, we told ourselves, it wasn't as though Oscar had died or got lost again—he had gone to a good family who would look after him. In fact he had really gone home.

And of course, we still had our much-loved Sam, although he didn't help in the early stages by sniffing disconsolately where Oscar's bed used to lie then collapsing on the rug with a long lugubrious sigh.

There was one other thing, too. I had a little notion forming in my mind, an idea which I would spring on Helen when the time was right. It was about a month after that shattering night and we were coming out of the cinema at Brawton at the end of our half day. I looked at my watch.

"Only eight o'clock," I said. "How about going to see Oscar?"

Helen looked at me in surprise. "You mean—drive on to Wederly?"

"Yes, it's only about five miles."

A smile crept slowly across her face. "That would be lovely. But do you think they would mind?"

"The Gibbons? No, I'm sure they wouldn't. Let's go."

Wederly was a big village and the ploughman's cottage was at the far end a few yards beyond the Methodist chapel. I pushed open the garden gate and we walked down the path.

A busy-looking little woman answered my knock. She was drying her hands on a striped towel.

"Mrs Gibbons?" I said.

"Aye, that's me."

"I'm James Herriot—and this is my wife."

Her eyes widened uncomprehendingly. Clearly the name meant nothing to her.

"We had your cat for a while," I added.

Suddenly she grinned and waved her towel at us. "Oh aye, ah remember now. Sep told me about you. Come in, come in!"

The big kitchen-living room was a tableau of life with six children and thirty shillings a week. Battered furniture, rows of much-mended washing on a pulley, black cooking range and a general air of chaos.

Sep got up from his place by the fire, put down his newspaper, took off a pair of steel-rimmed spectacles and shook hands.

He waved Helen to a sagging armchair. "Well, it's right nice to see you. Ah've often spoke of ye to t'missis."

His wife hung up her towel. "Yes, and I'm glad to meet ye both. I'll get some tea in a minnit."

She laughed and dragged a bucket of muddy water into a corner. "I've been washin' football jerseys. Them lads just handed them to me tonight—as if I haven't enough to do."

As she ran the water into the kettle, I peeped surreptitiously around me and I noticed Helen doing the same. But we searched in vain. There was no sign of a cat. Surely he couldn't have run away again? With a growing feeling of dismay, I realized that my little scheme could backfire devastatingly.

It wasn't until the tea had been made and poured that I dared to raise the subject.

"How—" I asked diffidently. "How is—er—Tiger?"

"Oh, he's grand," the little woman replied briskly. She glanced up at the clock on the mantelpiece. "He should be back any time now, then you'll be able to see 'im."

As she spoke, Sep raised a finger. "Ah think ah can hear 'im now."

He walked over and opened the door and our Oscar strode in with all his old grace and majesty. He took one look at Helen and leaped on to her lap. With a cry of delight she put down her cup and stroked the beautiful fur as the cat arched himself against her hand and the familiar purr echoed round the room.

"He knows me," she murmured. "He knows me."

Sep nodded and smiled. "He does that. You were good to 'im. He'll never forget ye, and we won't either, will we mother?"

"No, we won't, Mrs Herriot," his wife said as she applied butter to a slice of gingerbread. "That was a kind thing ye did for us and I 'ope you'll come and see us all whenever you're near."

"Well, thank you," I said. "We'd love to—we're often in Brawton."

I went over and tickled Oscar's chin, then I turned again to Mrs Gibbons. "By the way, it's after nine o'clock. Where has he been till now?"

She poised her butter knife and looked into space.

"Let's see, now," she said. "It's Thursday, isn't it? Ah yes, it's 'is night for the Yoga class."

RIDDLE

Ian Serraillier

In the dripping gloom I see
A creature with broad antlers,
Motionless it turns its head;
One gleaming eye devours the dark.
I hear it cough and clear its throat;
Then, with a hungry roar it charges into the night
And is swallowed whole.

(a motorcycle)

Who Am I?

Felice Holman

The trees ask me,
And the sky,
And the sea asks me
Who am I?

The grass asks me,
And the sand,
And the rocks ask me
Who am I?

The wind tells me
At nightfall,
And the rain tells me
Someone small.

Someone small
Someone small
But a piece
of
it
all.

The Scotty Who Knew Too Much

James Thurber

Several summers ago there was a Scotty who went to the country for a visit. He decided that all the farm dogs were cowards, because they were afraid of a certain animal that had a white stripe down its back. "You are a pussycat and I can lick you," the Scotty said to the farm dog who lived in the house where the Scotty was visiting. "I can lick the little animal with the white stripe, too. Show him to me."

"Don't you want to ask any questions about him?" said the farm dog.

"Nah," said the Scotty. "*You* ask the questions."

So the farm dog took the Scotty into the woods and showed him the white-striped animal and the Scotty closed in on him, growling and slashing. It was all over in a moment and the Scotty lay on his back. When he came to, the farm dog said, "What happened?"

"He threw vitriol," said the Scotty, "but he never laid a glove on me."

A few days later the farm dog told the Scotty there was another animal all the farm dogs were afraid of. "Lead me to him," said the Scotty. "I can lick anything that doesn't wear horseshoes."

"Don't you want to ask any questions about him?" said the farm dog.

"Nah," said the Scotty. "Just show me where he hangs out." So the farm dog led him to a place in the woods and pointed out the little animal when he came along. "A clown," said the Scotty, "a pushover," and he closed in, leading with his left and exhibiting some mighty fancy footwork. In less than a second, the Scotty was flat on his back, and when he woke up the farm dog was pulling quills out of him.

"What happened?" said the farm dog.

"He pulled a knife on me," said the Scotty, "but at least I have learned how you fight out here in the country, and now I am going to beat you up." So he closed in on the farm dog, holding his nose with one front paw to ward off the vitriol and covering his eyes with the other front paw to keep out the knives. The Scotty couldn't see his opponent and he couldn't smell his opponent and he was so badly beaten that he had to be taken back to the city and put in a nursing home.

Moral: *It is better to ask some questions than to know all the answers.*

The Dog That Talked

Traditional

A man was entering a village inn one day, when a large sheepdog lying beside the door looked up, and said to him, "Good morning, sir." The man stopped in astonishment, thinking he must be mistaken, but the dog said again, "Good morning, sir."

"Er—good morning," he managed to reply, and going indoors, he said to the landlord, "That's an extraordinary dog of yours just outside."

"Oh, I don't know, sir," answered the man, "I don't know there's anything special about him."

"Nothing special!" exclaimed the other. "He said 'Good morning, sir' to me as I came in."

"Impossible!" said the landlord. "But he did—he said it twice." "Oh, no, sir, you must be mistaken," said the man again. Then, after a pause, he asked, "Was there another dog there as well?" "I don't think so," said the guest; "but wait a minute. There was a little white terrier, but he was lying quite a way off."

"Ah! that'd be it," the landlord said. "He's a ventriloquist!"

28

exerpt from *Sounder*

William H. Armstrong

Sounder is the story of a poor Southern black family in the 1930's and their loyal dog. The father of the family has been put on a chain gang for stealing food, and the son has spent time each year traveling the countryside searching for him. The dog, Sounder, got his name from his deep, rich bark, but he hasn't used his voice except to whine since his master was arrested. At that time, Sounder was shot while trying to protect his master. When this selection opens, the son has just made the acquaintance of a schoolteacher who offers to educate him.

"Who's been kindly to your hurts?" the boy's mother asked as she looked down at the clean white rags that bandaged the boy's fingers. Rocking on the porch, she had seen the white dog swinging back and forth in the sun when the boy wasn't much more than a moving spot far down the road. "For a while I wasn't sure it was you," she said. "Why you walkin' fast? You done found him? Is your hand hurt bad? Is that a Bible some body's done mistreated?" The woman's eyes had come to rest on the book the boy held in his good hand.

"No. It's a book. I found it in a trash can."

"Be careful what you carry off, child," his mother said. "It can cause a heap o' trouble."

"I got somethin' to tell," the boy said as he sat down on the edge of the porch and ran his bandaged fingers over the head of the great coon dog who had stopped his jumping and whining and lay at the boy's feet with his head cocked to the side, looking up with his one eye. The younger children sat in a line beside the boy, waiting to hear.

"Is he poorly?" the woman asked slowly. "Is he far?"

"It's about somethin' else," the boy said after a long spell of quiet. "I ain't found him yet."

The boy told his mother and the children about his night in the teacher's cabin. The teacher wanted him to come back and go to school. He had been asked to live in the teacher's cabin and do his chores. The children's eyes widened when they heard the cabin had two lamps, two stoves, and grass growing in a yard with a fence and a gate. He told how the teacher could read and that there were lots of books on shelves in the cabin. "Maybe he will write letters to the road camps for you," the mother said, " 'cause you'll be so busy with schoolin' and cleanin' the schoolhouse for him that you can't go searchin' no more."

"Maybe I'd have time," the boy said. "But he says like you, 'Better not to go. Just be patient and time will pass.' "

"It's all powerful puzzlin' and aggravatin', but it's the Lord's will." The boy noticed that his mother had stopped rocking; the loose boards did not rattle as the chair moved on them.

"The teacher said he'd walk all the way and reason about it if you didn't want me to come to him. You don't want me to go, but I'll come home often as I can. And sometime I might bring word."

"It's a sign; I believes in signs." The rocker began to move back and forth, rattling the loose boards in the porch floor. "Go child. The Lord has come to you."

When he returned to the cabin with books on the shelves and the kind man with the white hair and the gentle voice, all the boy carried was his book with one cover missing—the book that he couldn't understand. In the summers he came home to take his father's place in the fields, for cabin rent had to be paid with field work. In the winter he seldom came because it took "more'n a day's walkin' and sleepin' on the ground."

"Ain't worth it" his mother would say.

Each year, after he had been gone for a whole winter and returned, the faithful Sounder would come hobbling on three legs far down the road to meet him. The great dog would wag his tail and whine. He never barked. The boy sang at his work in the fields, and his mother rocked in her chair and sang on the porch of the cabin. Sometimes when Sounder scratched fleas under the porch, she would look at the hunting lantern and the empty possum sack hanging against the wall. Six crops of persimmons and wild grapes had ripened. The possums and raccoons had gathered them unmolested. The lantern and possum sack hung untouched. "No use to nobody no more," the woman said.

The boy read to his brother and sisters when he had finished his day in the fields. He read the story of Joseph over and over and never wearied of it. "In all the books in the teacher's cabin, there's no story as good as Joseph's story" he would say to them.

The woman, listening and rocking, would say "The Lord has come to you, child. The Lord has certainly come to you."

Late one August afternoon the boy and his mother sat on the shaded corner of the porch. The heat and drought of dog days had parched the earth, and the crops had been laid by. The boy had come home early because there was nothing to do in the fields.

"Dog days is a terrible time," the woman said. "It's when the heat is so bad the dogs go mad." The boy would not tell her that the teacher had told him that dog days got their name from the Dog Star because it rose and set with the sun during that period. She had her own feeling for the earth, he thought, and he would not confuse it.

"It sure is hot," he said instead. "Lucky to come from the fields early." He watched the heat waves as they made the earth look like it was moving in little ripples.

Sounder came around the corner of the cabin from somewhere, hobbled back and forth as far as the road several times, and then went to his cool spot under the porch. "That's what I say about dog days," the woman said. "Poor creature's been addled with the heat for three days. Can't find no place to quiet down. Been down the road nearly out o' sight a second time today, and now he musta come from the fencerows. Whines all the time. A mad dog is a fearful sight. Slobberin' at the mouth and runnin' every which way 'cause they're blind. Have to shoot 'em 'fore they bite some child. It's awful hard."

"Sounder won't go mad," the boy said. "He's lookin' for a cooler spot, I reckon."

A lone figure came on the landscape as a speck and slowly grew into a ripply form through the heat waves. "Scorchin' to be walkin' and totin' far today," she said as she pointed to the figure on the road.

A catbird fussed in the wilted lilac at the corner of the cabin. "Why's that bird fussin' when no cat's prowlin? Old folks has a sayin' that if a catbird fusses 'bout nothin', somethin' bad is comin'. It's a bad sign."

"Sounder, I reckon," the boy said. "He just passed her bush when he came around the cabin."

In the tall locust at the edge of the fence, its top leaves yellowed from lack of water, a mockingbird mimicked the catbird with half a dozen notes, decided it was too hot to sing, and disappeared. The great coon dog, whose rhythmic panting came through the porch floor, came from under the house and began to whine.

As the figure on the road drew near, it took shape and grew indistinct again in the wavering heat. Sometimes it seemed to be a person dragging something, for little puffs of red dust rose in sulfurous clouds at every other step. Once or twice they thought it might be a brown cow or mule, dragging its hooves in the sand and raising and lowering its weary head.

Sounder panted faster, wagged his tail, whined, moved from the dooryard to the porch and back to the dooryard.

The figure came closer. Now it appeared to be a child carrying something on its back and limping.

"The children still at the creek?" she asked.

"Yes, but it's about dry."

Suddenly the voice of the great coon hound broke the sultry August deadness. The dog dashed along the road, leaving three-pointed clouds of red dust to settle back to earth behind him. The mighty voice rolled out upon the valley, each flutelike bark echoing from slope to slope.

"Lord's mercy! Dog days done made him mad." And the rocker was still.

Sounder was a young dog again. His voice was the same mellow sound that had ridden the November breeze from the lowlands to the hills. The boy and his mother looked at each other. The catbird stopped her fussing in the wilted lilac bush. On three legs, the dog moved with the same lightning speed that had carried him to the throat of a grounded raccoon.

Sounder's master had come home. Taking what might have been measured as a halting half step and then pulling a stiff, dead leg forward, dragging a foot turned sideways in the dust, the man limped into the yard. Sounder seemed to understand that to jump up and put his paw against his master's breast would topple him into the dust, so the great dog smelled and whined and wagged his tail and licked the limp hand dangling at his master's side. He hopped wildly around his master in a circle that almost brought head and tail together.

The head of the man was pulled to the side where a limp arm dangled and where the foot pointed outward as it was dragged through the dust. What had been a shoulder was now pushed up and back to make a one-sided hump so high that the leaning head seemed to rest upon it. The mouth was askew too, and the voice came out of the part farthest away from the withered, wrinkled, lifeless side.

The woman in the still rocker said, "Lord, Lord," and sat suffocated in shock.

"Sounder knew it was you just like you was comin' home from work," the boy said in a clear voice.

Half the voice of the man was gone too, so in slow, measured, stuttering he told how he had been caught in a dynamite blast in the prison quarry, how the dead side had been crushed under an avalanche of limestone, and

33

how he had been missed for a whole night in the search for dead and wounded. He told how the pain of the crushing stone had stopped in the night, how doctors had pushed and pulled and encased the numb side of his body in a cast, how they had spoken kindly to him and told him he would die. But he resolved he would not die, even with a half-dead body, because he wanted to come home again.

"For being hurt, they let me have time off my sentence," the man said, "and since I couldn't work, I guess they was glad to."

"The Lord has brought you home," the woman said.

The boy heard faint laughter somewhere behind the cabin. The children were coming home from the creek. He went around the cabin slowly, then hurried to meet them.

"Pa's home," he said and grabbed his sister, who had started to run toward the cabin. "Wait. He's mighty crippled up, so behave like nothin' has happened."

"Can he walk?" the youngest child asked.

"Yes! And don't you ask no questions."

"You been mighty natural and considerate," the mother said to the younger children later when she went to the woodpile and called them to pick dry kindling for a quick fire. When she came back to the porch she said, "We was gonna just have a cold piece 'cause it's so sultry, but now I think I'll cook."

Everything don't change much, the boy thought. There's eatin' and sleepin' and talkin' and settin' that goes on. One day might be different from another, but there ain't much difference when they're put together.

Sometimes there were long quiet spells. Once or twice the boy's mother said to the boy, "He's powerful proud of your learnin'. Read somethin' from the Scriptures." But mostly they just talked about heat and cold, and wind and clouds, and what's gonna be done, and time passing.

As the days of August passed and September brought signs of autumn, the crippled man sat on the porch step and leaned the paralyzed, deformed side of his body against a porch post. This was the only comfortable sitting position he could find. The old coon dog would lie facing his master, with his one eye fixed and his one ear raised. Sometimes he would tap his tail against the earth.

Sometimes the ear would droop and the eye would close. Then the great muscles would flex in dreams of the hunt, and the mighty chest would give off the muffled whisper of a bark. Sometimes the two limped together to the edge of the fields, or wandered off into the pine woods. They never went along the road. Perhaps they knew how strange a picture they made when they walked together.

About the middle of September the boy left to go back to his teacher. "It's the most important thing," his mother said.

And the crippled man said, "We're fine. We won't need nothin'."

"I'll come for a few days before it's cold to help gather wood and walnuts."

The broken body of the old man withered more and more, but when the smell of harvest and the hunt came with October, his spirit seemed to quicken his dragging step. One day he cleaned the dusty lantern globe, and the old dog, remembering, bounced on his three legs and wagged his tail as if to say "I'm ready."

The boy had come home. To gather the felled trees and chop the standing dead ones was part of the field pay too. He had been cutting and dragging timber all day.

Sometimes he had looked longingly at the lantern and possum sack, but something inside him had said "Wait. Wait and go together." But the boy did not want to go hunting anymore. And without his saying anything, his father had said, "You're too tired, child. We ain't goin' far, no way."

In the early darkness the halting, hesitant swing of the lantern marked the slow path from fields to pine woods toward the lowlands. The boy stood on the porch, watching until the light was lost behind pine branches. Then he went and sat by the stove. His mother rocked as the mound of kernels grew in the fold of her apron. "He been mighty peart," she said. "I hope he don't fall in the dark. Maybe he'll be happy now he can go hunting again." And she took up her singing where she had left off.

Ain't nobody else gonna walk it for you,
You gotta walk it by yourself.

36

*It matters not how long we live,
but how.*

I May Be Silent, But

Tsuboi Shigeji

Translated by Geoffrey Bownas and
Anthony Thwaite

I may be silent, but
I'm thinking.
I may not talk, but
Don't mistake me for a wall.

exerpt from

ZEELY

•

Virginia Hamilton

Elizabeth Perry and her younger brother John are spending the summer with their Uncle Ross on his farm. Elizabeth has a vivid imagination. She has renamed herself Geeder and her brother Toeboy for the summer. Geeder is eager to exercise the authority she feels her father gave her when he put her on the train and said, "And now, I leave it all to you."

The first day at the farm, Geeder and Toeboy looked over the hogs in Uncle Ross' west field. These were no ordinary animals, but prize razorback hogs owned by a Mr. Nat Tayber and his daughter, who rented the land from Uncle Ross.

"Look at the size of those hogs!" Toeboy said.

"They're big, all right," Geeder said, "and they're mean. I wouldn't get too close to them even if I had to."

They leaned on the fence, looking in at the hogs. The hogs wallowed around, eating and rutting in the earth with their snouts. Often they came close to the fence but veered away as they caught the scent of Geeder and Toeboy.

"Let's go," said Geeder. "I don't believe they like us here."

They fed a bit of corn to Uncle Ross' two hundred leghorn chickens. They could feed them as much corn as they liked, Uncle Ross had said. And they could gather up eggs whenever they had a mind to.

"Well, it's the truth. I can do whatever I want," Geeder said to herself. Still, not one thing had taken place that fit with her father's words *"And now, I leave it all to you."*

That was why, when evening came, Geeder decided to spread sheets and blankets out on the front lawn. She and Toeboy would sleep outside and maybe they would see a comet.

Toeboy liked looking up into the sky, as long as Geeder was talking. The sound of her voice made the night less strange and he felt safe. He had made his bed partly beneath a sprawling lilac bush close to the house. Geeder had made hers near the high hedge that shielded the house from the road. Toeboy felt so good that he decided to get up and make his bed next to Geeder's.

"I think I'll come over there," he called to her.

"Better not," she said. "Just better stay where you are."

"But I want to sleep by the hedge, too," he said.

"I know one thing," Geeder said. "Late at night in the country, night travellers walk along dark roads."

"What?"

"Night travellers," Geeder said again, "and they usually come up when you're just about asleep."

"What kind of things are they?" asked Toeboy. He dug his legs deeper among the branches of the lilac bush.

"I'll tell you this," Geeder said. "If you see one, you'd better close your eyes fast and dive as far under the covers as you can go. They don't like kids watching them. In fact, they don't like anybody watching them!"

Toeboy stayed uneasily beneath the lilac bush. He was glad to be so near the house, for if he heard any sound, he could race inside. He did not mind at all seeing half stars and a half-moon through the lilac leaves.

Geeder turned around to see what Toeboy was doing and saw that he had pulled most of his bedding all the way under the lilac shrub. That nearly made her laugh out loud. She had made up the whole thing about the night travellers. She was only trying to frighten Toeboy—not for any really mean reason, but just because he was little and was easy to scare. As far as she knew, nobody walked late at night along this dark road.

But maybe ghosts do, she thought. A chill passed up her spine and she closed her eyes tight for an instant to make it go away.

"Toeboy," she called, "are you still awake?"

"I'm awake," he said. "I don't want to sleep yet." He lay fingering the cool leaves of the lilac.

"Then I'll tell you all about stars," said Geeder, "since you're so wide awake."

Geeder talked about the stars and the night. She knew Toeboy had gone to sleep when he no longer asked her anything or chuckled about what she said.

A long time passed. Geeder dozed and awoke with a start. The grass beyond the tip of her toes was wet with dew. She pulled the blankets more tightly around her, tucking her feet safely inside. She had closed her eyes again when she heard a rustling sound on Leadback Road.

Some old animal, she thought. The sound grew louder and she could not think what it was. Suddenly, what she had told Toeboy flashed through her mind.

Night travellers! She dove under the covers.

But something's happening! she told herself, poking her head out again.

It took all her courage to crawl out of the covers and the few feet over the wet grass up to the hedge. She trembled with fear but peeked through the hedge in spite of it. What she saw made her bend low, hugging the ground for protection. Truthfully, she wasn't sure what she saw. The branches of the hedge didn't allow much of a view.

Something tall and white was moving down the road. It didn't quite touch the ground. Geeder could hear no sound of footsteps. She couldn't see its head or arms. Beside it and moving with it was something that squeaked ominously. The white, very long figure made a rustling sound when she held her breath. It passed by toward town.

Geeder watched, moving her head ever so slowly until she could no longer see it. After waiting for what seemed hours, quaking at each sound and murmur of the night,

42

she crept back to bed, pulling the covers over her eyes. She lay, cold and scared, unable to think and afraid even to clear her dry throat. This way, she fell asleep. She awoke in the morning, refreshed but stiff in every muscle.

Geeder lay for a moment, watching mist rise from the pink, sweet clover that sprinkled the lawn. The air smelled clean and fresh and was not yet hot from the sun.

"I've got to decide," she whispered. In the stillness, the sound of her own voice startled her. She turned carefully around to see if Toeboy had stirred. The tangled bedding deep in the lilac bush did not move.

"If I tell Toeboy about the night traveller," she whispered, "he might not want to sleep outside any more. Just think of it! Not more than a few hours ago, an awful, spooky thing walked by here!"

Geeder wasn't at all sure she wanted to sleep outside again, herself.

"Goodness knows what a night traveller will do if it sees you watching! Maybe I'd better tell Uncle Ross. . . . Maybe I shouldn't."

Geeder knew it would take her a while to figure out what course to take. Almost any minute now, the people Uncle Ross rented land to would come down the road. Uncle Ross had said they came every morning as soon as the sun was well up in the sky. It was just about time, and watching them would be something to do.

When her dew-soaked blankets grew warm from the sun, Geeder whistled for Toeboy as softly as she could. Turning around, she saw one eye peek out from the lilac bush.

"Wake up, Toeboy!" she whispered loudly. "I think I hear them coming!"

Toeboy leaped up before he looked where he was going and hit his head against a branch. Leaves spilled dew all over him. He was wet and still half asleep when Geeder yanked him to the ground before they could be seen.

They knelt low by the hedge. Trying not to move or blink an eye, they watched Mr. Tayber and his daughter come into view along Leadback Road. What they saw was no ordinary sight. They watched, spellbound, for nothing

in the world could have prepared them for the sight of Miss Zeely Tayber.

Zeely Tayber was more than six and a half feet tall, thin and deeply dark as a pole of Ceylon ebony. She wore a long smock that reached to her ankles. Her arms, hands and feet were bare, and her thin, oblong head didn't seem to fit quite right on her shoulders.

She had very high cheekbones and her eyes seemed to turn inward on themselves. Geeder couldn't say what expression she saw on Zeely's face. She knew only that it was calm, that it had pride in it, and that the face was the most beautiful she had ever seen.

Zeely's long fingers looked exactly like bean pods left a long time in the sun.

Geeder wanted to make sure Toeboy noticed Zeely's hands but the Taybers were too close, and she was afraid they would hear her.

Mr. Tayber and Zeely carried feed pails, which made a grating sound. It was the only sound on the road besides that of Mr. Tayber's heavy footsteps. Zeely made no sound at all.

You would think she would, thought Geeder, she was so long and tall.

Geeder and Toeboy stayed quiet as the Taybers passed, and the Taybers gave no sign that they saw them hiding there. Uncle Ross had said that they were not known to speak much, even to one another. They had not lived in Crystal always, as Uncle Ross had.

Geeder and Toeboy watched the Taybers until they went out of sight. It was then that Toeboy said, "Let's go watch them in the field."

"No," said Geeder quietly, "no, Toeboy." She could not possibly have made him understand how stunned she had been at seeing Miss Zeely Tayber for the first time. Never in her life had she seen anyone quite like her.

Later on, as they fed the chickens, Geeder talked to Toeboy about the arrival of the Taybers in Crystal.

"They must have come early one morning," she told him. "They might have come from the west but I suspect they came from Tallahassee. They brought all their wild animals with them in a wagon train and they bought that house they live in from Mr. Crawley."

"How could they come in a wagon train?" Toeboy wanted to know. Geeder was thinking and didn't answer him.

"Mr. Tayber came down the road to see about using some of the west field," Geeder said. "Uncle Ross was to get a third of the profit from the sale of the best razorback hogs."

"But why would Uncle Ross rent land to strangers?" Toeboy asked. "And what is 'a third of the profit'?"

"Oh, goodness, Toeboy!" Geeder said. "I don't know what 'a third of the profit' would be. And if Uncle Ross waited until he got to know the Taybers the way you know ordinary people, he'd wait forever. Listen." She stood very close to Toeboy, as though the chickens might hear and she didn't want them to. "All of Crystal knows only a few things about the Taybers."

"What things?" Toeboy asked.

"Well, they know that Zeely Tayber is awfully tall for a girl. Even Nat Tayber is very tall," Geeder said, "but not too tall for a grown man."

"What else do they know?" asked Toeboy.

"The Taybers like to be left alone," Geeder said, counting off on her fingers. "Zeely's mother is dead. Both Nat and Zeely have thin noses and very high cheekbones."

"Maybe the Taybers are Indians," Toeboy said.

Geeder had to laugh. "The Taybers are colored people," she said, "just like you and me and Uncle Ross. But they are different from any people I've ever seen. We don't know what kind of person Zeely is." Geeder's voice was full of the awe she felt for her. "But you know what I think? I think we've found a new people that nobody's ever heard of!"

All that morning, Geeder talked to Toeboy about Zeely. When they sat down for lunch with Uncle Ross, Toeboy was surprised by the off-handed way Geeder asked, "How long have those Tayber people been around this town?"

"Oh, it's been about a year and a half now," Uncle Ross said.

"That's a long time," Geeder said. "I guess you've gotten to know Mr. Tayber and his girl real well in all that time."

Uncle Ross smiled. "No," he said, "I wouldn't say that. The Taybers aren't easy to know, although they are speaking-polite to most folks."

"What would you say then?" asked Toeboy.

"What would I say when?" Uncle Ross replied.

Geeder wished Toeboy would just keep quiet. "He means to say that if you don't know them well, then what way *do* you know them?" she asked. "And why don't you know them well when they're in the west field every day working over those animals?"

Uncle Ross took a careful look at Toeboy and a much longer look at Geeder.

"Toeboy means to say all that?" he said to Geeder. "Well, I mean to say just what I did say. Mr. Tayber and his daughter live to themselves. They stay aloof from the whole town." He paused. "One day, the town had no thought of them. The next day, there they were, hammering and putting storm windows in that old house once owned by Jacob Crawley."

"Just like that?" Geeder said, snapping her fingers.

"No, not exactly like that," Uncle Ross said. "Now that I think about it, there had been time . . . room . . . for people like them among us. It's like it took them a long time to get here. The first time we see them, they are taking care to fix up that house. Strangers. And they stay on taking their time, still strangers. That's all right, the way I see it."

"Strangers," Geeder said. But that was all she said. She asked no more questions.

But by nightfall, Geeder was ready to talk about Zeely Tayber once more. As she and Toeboy lay in their beds on the lawn, she began.

"You would think a lady like Zeely would have all kinds of friends," Geeder said. "I mean, being so tall and

47

being so pretty. But there she goes with just old Mr. Tayber. She hardly even talks to *him*."

"He doesn't talk much to her, either," Toeboy said.

"That's because both Zeely and Mr. Tayber are different," Geeder said, "with ways about them none of us can understand."

Toeboy lay beneath the lilac bush, hugging the covers around himself. He listened to the rise and fall of Geeder's voice and was lulled into a deep sleep.

Geeder stopped talking. She was watching the stars when there grew in her mind a lovely picture. . . . It was daytime, with sunlight spilling over Uncle Ross' farm. She sat in shade on a grassy slope beside Leadback Road. Miss Zeely Tayber came gliding down the road. Her face and arms were shiny from heat and walking so long in the sun. She came right up to Geeder. She had been looking for her.

"Geeder, have you waited long?" Miss Zeely said. "I would dearly love a drink of water from the pump room."

Geeder brought Miss Zeely a drink of water in a tall glass, and a silk handkerchief. Miss Zeely sat beside Geeder, sipping the water. She wiped her face with the handkerchief and then dried her hands. When she had finished, she folded the hanky and placed it in Geeder's palm.

"Geeder Perry," said Miss Zeely, "I don't know what I would do without you."

Geeder pretended she hadn't done anything at all. . . .

"Miss Zeely Tayber," she whispered to the stars, "oh, Miss Zeely!"

Her hand touched something cool and heavy beside her. Uncle Ross' flashlight! She had taken it from his workroom. She meant to shine the light on the night traveller just as it passed by the house.

Suddenly alert and watchful, she listened to the silence around her.

"If the night traveller tries to bother me, I'll throw the flashlight at it," she muttered. "And if that doesn't stop it, I'll scream and wake up the whole town!"

But Geeder was tricked by the fresh night air into

falling asleep. Many times she roused herself but did not awaken. Once she said in her sleep, "Is that you? Is that you coming?" It seemed that a voice came through the hedge, murmuring, "Yes, child, now sleep." It was her mother's voice. She slept more calmly then. She dreamed of home and people she knew there. In the morning, she was mad as a bull at having fallen asleep and had no recollection of the dream.

Grandpa and the Statue

Arthur Miller

Characters

Characters in the present time of the play:

ANNOUNCER
AUGUST
MONAGHAN (Young Monaghan, a soldier)

Characters from the past, heard in the flashback scenes which Young Monaghan remembers:

SHEEAN
MONAGHAN
CHILD MONAGHAN
NEIGHBORHOOD CHILDREN (Young Monaghan's friends):
GEORGE
JACK
JOE
CHARLEY
MIKE

Passengers on the Statue of Liberty boat:

ALF
GIRL
YOUNG MAN
MEGAPHONE VOICE
VETERAN (visitor to the Statue)

(*Music: Theme.*)

ANNOUNCER: The scene is the fourth floor of a giant army hospital overlooking New York Harbor. A young man sitting in a wheel chair is looking out a window—just looking. After a while another young man in another wheel chair rolls over to him and they both look. (*Music out.*)

AUGUST: You want to play some checkers with me, Monaghan?

MONAGHAN: Not right now.

AUGUST: Okay. (*Slight pause.*) You don't want to go feeling blue, Monaghan.

MONAGHAN: I'm not blue.

AUGUST: All you do most days is sit here looking out this window.

MONAGHAN: What do you want me to do, jump rope?

AUGUST: No, but what do you get out of it?

MONAGHAN: It's a beautiful view. Some companies make millions of dollars just printing that view on postcards.

AUGUST: Yeh, but nobody keeps looking at a postcard six, seven hours a day.

MONAGHAN: I come from around here; it reminds me of things. My young days.

AUGUST: That's right, you're Brooklyn, aren't you?

MONAGHAN: My house is only about a mile away.

AUGUST: That so. Tell me, are you looking at just the water all the time? I'm curious. I don't get a kick out of this view.

MONAGHAN: There's the Statue of Liberty out there. Don't you see it?

AUGUST: Oh, that's it. Yeh, that's nice to look at.

MONAGHAN: I like it. Reminds me of a lot of laughs.

AUGUST: Laughs? The Statue of Liberty?

MONAGHAN: Yeh, my grandfather. He got all twisted up with the Statue of Liberty.

AUGUST *(laughs a little)*: That so? What happened?

MONAGHAN: Well. My grandfather was the stingiest man in Brooklyn. "Mercyless" Monaghan, they used to call him. He even used to save umbrella handles.

AUGUST: What for?

MONAGHAN: Just couldn't stand seeing anything go to waste. After a big windstorm there'd be a lot of broken umbrellas lying around in the streets.

AUGUST: Yeh?

MONAGHAN: He'd go around picking them up. In our house the closets were always full of umbrella handles. My grandma used to say that he would go across the Brooklyn Bridge on the trolley just because he could come back on the same nickel. See, if you stayed on the trolley they'd let you come back for the same nickel.

AUGUST: What'd he do, just go over and come back?

MONAGHAN: Yeh, it made him feel good. Savin' money. Two and a half cents.

AUGUST: So how'd he get twisted up with the Statue of Liberty?

MONAGHAN: Well, way back in 1887 around there they were living on Butler Street. Butler Street, Brooklyn, practically runs right down to the river. One day he's sitting on the front porch, reading a paper he borrowed from the neighbors, when along comes this man Jack Sheean who lived up the block.

(Music: Sneak into above speech, then bridge, then out.)

SHEEAN *(slight brogue)*: A good afternoon to you, Monaghan.

MONAGHAN *(grandfather)*: How're you, Sheean, how're ya?

SHEEAN: Fair, fair. And how's Mrs. Monaghan these days?

MONAGHAN: Warm. Same as everybody else in summer.

SHEEAN: I've come to talk to you about the fund, Monaghan.

MONAGHAN: What fund is that?

SHEEAN: The Statue of Liberty fund.

MONAGHAN: Oh, that.

SHEEAN: It's time we come to grips with the subject, Monaghan.

MONAGHAN: I'm not interested, Sheean.

SHEEAN: Now hold up on that a minute. Let me tell you the facts. This here Frenchman has gone and built a fine Statue of Liberty. It costs the Lord knows how many millions to build. All they're askin' us to do is contribute enough to put up a base for the statue to stand on.

MONAGHAN: I'm not . . . !

SHEEAN: Before you answer me. People all over the whole United States are puttin' in for it. Butler Street is doin' the same. We'd like to hang up a flag on the corner saying—"Butler Street, Brooklyn, is one hundred percent behind the Statue of Liberty." And Butler Street *is* a hundred percent subscribed except for you. Now will you give us a dime, Monaghan? One dime and we can put up the flag. Now what do you say to that?

MONAGHAN: I'm not throwin' me good money away for somethin' I don't even know exists.

SHEEAN: Now what do you mean by that?

MONAGHAN: Have you seen this statue?

SHEEAN: No, but it's in a warehouse. And as soon as we get the money to build the pedestal they'll take it and put it up on that island in the river, and all the boats

comin' in from the old country will see it there and it'll
raise the hearts of the poor immigrants to see such a
fine sight on their first look at this country.

MONAGHAN: And how do I know it's in this here
warehouse at all?

SHEEAN: You read your paper, don't you? It's been in all
the papers for the past year.

MONAGHAN: Ha, the papers! Last year I read in the paper
that they were about to pave Butler Street and take out
all the holes. Turn around and look at Butler Street,
Mr. Sheean.

SHEEAN: All right. I'll do this: I'll take you to the
warehouse and show you the statue. Will you give me
a dime then?

MONAGHAN: Well . . . I'm not sayin' I would, and I'm not
sayin' I wouldn't. But I'd be more *likely* if I saw the
thing large as life, I would.

SHEEAN (*peeved*): All right, then. Come along. (*Music up and down and out.*) (*Footsteps, in a warehouse . . . echo . . . they come to a halt.*) Now then. Do you see the Statue of Liberty or don't you see it?

MONAGHAN: I see it all right, but it's all broke!

SHEEAN: *Broke!* They brought it from France on a boat. They had to take it apart, didn't they?

MONAGHAN: You got a secondhand statue, that's what you got, and I'm not payin' for new when they've shipped us something that's all smashed to pieces.

SHEEAN: Now just a minute, just a minute. Visualize what I'm about to tell you, Monaghan, get the picture of it. When this statue is put together it's going to stand ten stories high. Could they get a thing ten stories high into a four-story building such as this is? Use your good sense, now Monaghan.

MONAGHAN: What's that over there?

SHEEAN: Where?

MONAGHAN: That tablet there in her hand. What's it say? July Eye Vee (IV) MDCCLXXVI . . . what . . . what's all that?

SHEEAN: That means July 4, 1776. It's in Roman numbers. Very high class.

MONAGHAN: What's the good of it? If they're going to put a sign on her they ought to put on it: Welcome All. That's it. Welcome All.

SHEEAN: They decided July 4, 1776, and July 4, 1776, it's going to be!

MONAGHAN: All right, then let them get their dime from somebody else!

SHEEAN: Monaghan!

MONAGHAN: No, sir! I'll tell you something. I didn't think there was a statue but there is. She's all broke, it's true, but she's here and maybe they can get her together. But even if they do, will you tell me what sort of a welcome to immigrants it'll be, to have a gigantic thing like that in the middle of the river and in her hand is July Eye Vee MCDVC . . . whatever it is?

SHEEAN: That's the date the country was made!

MONAGHAN: The divil with the date! A man comin' in from

the sea wants a place to stay, not a date. When I come from the old country I git off at the dock and there's a feller says to me, "Would you care for a room for the night?" "I would that," I sez, and he sez, "All right then, follow me." He takes me to a rooming house. I no sooner sign me name on the register—which I was able to do even at that time—when I look around and the feller is gone clear away and took my valise in the bargain. A statue anyway can't move off so fast, but if she's going to welcome let her say welcome, not this MCDC. . . .

SHEEAN: All right, then, Monaghan. But all I can say is, you've laid a disgrace on the name of Butler Street. I'll put the dime in for ya.

MONAGHAN: Don't connect me with it! It's a swindle, is all it is. In the first place, it's broke; in the second place, if they do put it up, it'll come down with the first high wind that strikes it.

SHEEAN: The engineers say it'll last forever!

MONAGHAN: And I say it'll topple into the river in a high wind! Look at the inside of her. She's all hollow!

SHEEAN: I've heard everything now, Monaghan. Just about everything. Goodbye.

MONAGHAN: What do you mean, goodbye? How am I to get back to Butler Street from here?

SHEEAN: You've got legs to walk.

MONAGHAN: I'll remind you that I come on the trolley.

SHEEAN: And I'll remind you that I paid your fare and I'm not repeating the kindness.

MONAGHAN: Sheean? You've stranded me!

(*Music up and down.*)

YOUNG MONAGHAN: That was grandpa. That's why I have to laugh every time I look at the statue now.

AUGUST: Did he ever put the dime in?

YOUNG MONAGHAN: Well—in a way. What happened was this: His daughters got married and finally my mom . . . put *me* out on Butler Street. I got to be pretty attached to grandpa. He'd even give me an umbrella handle and make a sword out of it for me. Naturally, I wasn't very old before he began working on me about the statue.

56

(High wind.)

CHILD MONAGHAN *(softly, as though grandpa is in bed)*: Grampa?

MONAGHAN *(awakened)*: Heh? What are you doin' up?

CHILD MONAGHAN: Ssssh! Listen!

(Wind rising up and fading. Rising higher and fading.)

MONAGHAN *(gleefully)*: Aaaaaaaah! Yes, yes. This'll do it, boy. This'll do it! First thing in the morning we'll go down to the docks, and I'll bet you me life that Mr. Sheean's statue is smashed down and lyin' on the bottom of the bay. Go to sleep now, and we'll have a look first thing.

(*Music up and down.*)

(*Footsteps.*)

CHILD MONAGHAN: If it fell down, all the people will get their dimes back, won't they, grampa? Slow down, I can't walk so fast.

MONAGHAN: Not only will they get their dimes back, but Mr. Sheean and the whole crew that engineered the collection are going to rot in jail. Now mark my words. Here, now, we'll take a short cut around this shed. . . .

(*Footsteps continue a moment, then gradually—disappointedly— they come to a halt.*)

CHILD MONAGHAN: She's . . . she's still standing, grampa.

MONAGHAN: She is that. (*Uncomprehending.*) I don't understand it. That was a terrible wind last night. Terrible.

CHILD MONAGHAN: Maybe she's weaker though. Heh?

MONAGHAN: Why . . . sure, that must be it. I'll wager she's hangin' by a thread. (*Realizing.*) Of course! That's why they put her out there in the water, so when she falls down she won't be flattening out a lot of poor innocent people. Hey—feel that?

CHILD MONAGHAN: The wind! It's starting to blow again!

MONAGHAN: Sure, and look at the sky blackening over! (*Wind rising.*) Feel it comin' up! Take your last look at the statue, boy. If I don't mistake me eyes she's takin' a small list to Jersey already!

(*Music up and down.*)

YOUNG MONAGHAN: It was getting embarrassing for me on the block. I kept promising the other kids that when the next wind came the statue would come down. We even had a game. Four or five kids would stand in a semicircle around one kid who was the statue. The statue kid had to stand on his heels and look right in our eyes. Then we'd all take a deep breath and blow in his face. He'd fall down like a stick of wood. They all believed me and grampa . . . until one day. We were standing around and throwing rocks at an old milk can . . .

(Banging of rocks against milk can.)

GEORGE *(kid)*: What're you doin?

CHILD MONAGHAN: What do we look like we're doin'?

GEORGE: I'm going someplace tomorrow.

CHARLEY *(kid)*: I know, church. Watch out, I'm throwin'.

(Can being hit)

GEORGE: I mean after church.

JACK: Where?

GEORGE: My old man's going to take me out on the Statue of Liberty boat.

(Banging against can abruptly stops.)

CHILD MONAGHAN: You're not going out on the statue, though, are you?

GEORGE: Sure, that's where we're going.

CHILD MONAGHAN: But you're liable to get killed. Supposing there's a high wind tomorrow?

GEORGE: My old man says that statue couldn't fall down if all the wind in the world and John L. Sullivan hit it at the same time.

CHILD MONAGHAN: Is that so?

GEORGE: Yeh, that's so. My old man says that the only reason your grandfather's saying that it's going to fall down is that he's ashamed he didn't put a dime in for the pedestal.

CHILD MONAGHAN: Is that so?

GEORGE: Yeh, that's so.

CHILD MONAGHAN: Well, you tell your old man that if he gets killed tomorrow not to come around to my grandfather and say he didn't warn him!

JACK: Hey, George, would your father take me along?

GEORGE: I'll ask him, maybe he——

CHILD MONAGHAN: What, are you crazy, Jack?

MIKE: Ask him if he'd take me too, will ya, George?

CHILD MONAGHAN: Mike, what's the matter with you?

JOE: Me too, George, I'll ask my mother for money.

CHILD MONAGHAN: Joe! Didn't you hear what my grampa said?

JOE: Well . . . I don't really believe that any more.

CHILD MONAGHAN: You don't be . . .

59

MIKE: Me neither.

JACK: I don't really think your grampa knows what he's talkin' about.

CHILD MONAGHAN: He don't, heh? *(Ready to weep.)* Okay. . . . Okay. *(Bursting out.)* I just hope that wind blows tomorrow, boy! I just hope that wind blows! *(Music up and down. Creaking of a rocking chair.)* Grampa . . . ?

MONAGHAN: Huh?

CHILD MONAGHAN: Can you stop rocking for a minute? *(Rocking stops.)* Can you put down your paper? *(Rustle of paper.)* I—I read the weather report for tomorrow.

MONAGHAN: The weather report . . .

CHILD MONAGHAN: Yeh. It says fair and cool.

MONAGHAN: What of it?

CHILD MONAGHAN: I was wondering. Supposing you and me we went on a boat tomorrow. You know, I see the water every day when I go down to the docks to play, but I never sat on it. I mean in a boat.

MONAGHAN: Oh. Well, we might take the ferry on the Jersey side. We might do that.

CHILD MONAGHAN: Yeh, but there's nothing to see in Jersey.

MONAGHAN: You can't go to Europe tomorrow.

CHILD MONAGHAN: No, but couldn't we go toward the ocean? Just . . . *toward* it?

MONAGHAN: Toward it. What—what is it on your mind, boy? What is it now?

CHILD MONAGHAN: Well, I . . .

MONAGHAN: Oh, you want to take the Staten Island ferry. Sure, that's in the direction of the sea.

CHILD MONAGHAN: No, grampa, not the Staten Island ferry.

MONAGHAN: You don't mean——*(Breaks off.)* Boy!

CHILD MONAGHAN: All the kids are going tomorrow with Georgie's old man.

MONAGHAN: You don't believe me any more.

CHILD MONAGHAN: I do, grampa, but . . .

MONAGHAN: You don't. If you did you'd stay clear of the Statue of Liberty for love of your life!

CHILD MONAGHAN: But, grampa, when is it going to fall down? All I do is wait and wait.

MONAGHAN (*with some uncertainty*): You've got to have faith.

CHILD MONAGHAN: But every kid in my class went to see it and now the ones that didn't are going tomorrow. And they all keep talking about it and all I do. . . . Well, I can't keep telling them it's a swindle. I—I wish we could see it, grampa. It don't cost so much to go.

MONAGHAN: As long as you put it that way, I'll have to admit I'm a bit curious meself as to how it's managed to stand upright so long. Tell you what I'll do. Barrin' wind, we'll chance it tomorrow!

CHILD MONAGHAN: Oh, gramp!

MONAGHAN: But! If anyone should ask you where we went you'll say—Staten Island. Are y' on?

CHILD MONAGHAN: Okay, sure. Staten Island.

MONAGHAN (*secretively*): We'll take the early boat, then. Mum's the word, now. For if old man Sheean hears that I went out there, I'll have no peace from the thief the rest of m' life.

(*Music up and down.*)

(*Boat whistles.*)

CHILD MONAGHAN: Gee, it's nice ridin' on a boat, ain't it, grampa?

MONAGHAN: Never said there was anything wrong with the boat. Boat's all right. You're sure now that Georgie's father is takin' the kids in the afternoon.

CHILD MONAGHAN: Yeh, that's when they're going. Gee, look at those two sea gulls. Wee!—look at them swoop! They caught a fish!

MONAGHAN: What I can't understand is what all these people see in that statue that they'll keep a boat like this full makin' the trip, year in and year out. To hear the newspapers talk, if the statue was gone we'd be at war with the nation that stole her the followin' mornin' early. All it is is a big high pile of French copper.

CHILD MONAGHAN: The teacher says it shows us that we got liberty.

MONAGHAN: Bah! If you've got liberty you don't need a statue to tell you you got it; and if you haven't got

61

liberty no statue's going to do you any good tellin' you you got it. It was a criminal waste of the people's money. *(Quietly.)* And just to prove it to you I'll ask this feller sitting right over there what he sees in it. You'll see what a madness the whole thing was. Say, mister?

ALF: Hey?

MONAGHAN: I beg your pardon. I'm a little strange here, and curious. Could you tell me why you're going to the Statue of Liberty?

ALF: Me? Well, I tell ya. I always wanted to take an ocean voyage. This is a pretty big boat—bigger than the ferries—so on Sundays, sometimes, I take the trip. It's better than nothing.

MONAGHAN: Thank you. *(To the boy.)* So much for the great meaning of that statue, me boy. We'll talk to this lady standing at the rail. I just want you to understand why I didn't give Sheean me dime. Madam, would you be good enough to . . . Oh pardon me. *(To boy.)* Better pass her by, she don't look so good. We'll ask that girl there. Young lady, if you'll pardon the curiosity of an old man . . . could you tell me in a few good words what it is about the statue that brings you out here?

GIRL: What statue?

MONAGHAN: Why, the Statue of Liberty up 'head. We're coming up to it.

GIRL: Statue of Liberty! Is this the Statue of Liberty boat?

MONAGHAN: Well, what'd you think it was?

GIRL: Oh, my! I'm supposed to be on the Staten Island ferry! Where's the ticket man? *(Going away.)* Ticket man! Where's the ticket man?

CHILD MONAGHAN: Gee whiz, nobody seems to want to see the statue.

MONAGHAN: Just to prove it, let's see this fellow sitting on this bench here. Young man, say . . .

YOUNG MAN: I can tell you in one word. For four days I haven't had a minute's peace. My kids are screaming, my wife is yelling, upstairs they play the piano all day long. The only place I can find that's quiet is a statue. That statue is my sweetheart. Every Sunday I beat it out to the island and sit next to her, and she don't talk.

CHILD MONAGHAN: I guess you were right, grampa. Nobody seems to think it means anything.

MONAGHAN: Not only doesn't mean anything, but if they'd used the money to build an honest roomin' house on that island, the immigrants would have a place to spend the night, their valises wouldn't get robbed, and they——

MEGAPHONE VOICE: *Please keep your seats while the boat is docking. Statue of Liberty—all out in five minutes!*

CHILD MONAGHAN: Look down there, gramp! There's a peanut stand! Could I have some?

MONAGHAN: I feel the wind comin' up. I don't think we dare take the time.

(Music up and down.)

CHILD MONAGHAN: Sssssseuuuuuww! Look how far you can see! Look at that ship way out in the ocean!

MONAGHAN: It is, it's quite a view. Don't let go of me hand now.

CHILD MONAGHAN: I betcha we could almost see California.

MONAGHAN: It's probably that grove of trees way out over there. They do say it's beyond Jersey.

CHILD MONAGHAN: Feels funny. We're standing right inside her head. Is that what you meant . . . July IV, MCD . . . ?

MONAGHAN: That's it. That tablet in her hand. Now shouldn't they have put Welcome All on it instead of that foreign language? Say! Do you feel her rockin'?

CHILD MONAGHAN: Yeah, she's moving a little bit. Listen, the wind!

(Whistling of wind.)

MONAGHAN: We better get down, come on! This way!

CHILD MONAGHAN: No, the stairs are this way! Come on!

(Running in echo. Then quick stop.)

MONAGHAN: No, I told you they're the other way! Come!

VETERAN *(calm, quiet voice)*: Don't get excited, pop. She'll stand.

MONAGHAN: She's swayin' awful.

VETERAN: That's all right. I been up here thirty, forty times. She gives with the wind, flexible. Enjoy the view, go on.

MONAGHAN: Did you say you've been up here forty times?

VETERAN: About that many.

MONAGHAN: What do you find here that's so interesting?

VETERAN: It calms my nerves.

MONAGHAN: Ah. It seems to me it would make you more nervous than you were.

VETERAN: No, not me. It kinda means something to me.

MONAGHAN: Might I ask what?

VETERAN: Well . . . I was in the Philippine War . . . back in '98. Left my brother back there.

MONAGHAN: Oh, yes. Sorry I am to hear it. Young man, I suppose, eh?

VETERAN: Yeh. We were both young. This is his birthday today.

MONAGHAN: Oh, I understand.

VETERAN: Yeh, this statue is about the only stone he's got. In my mind I feel it is anyway. This statue kinda looks like what we believe. You know what I mean?

MONAGHAN: Looks like what we believe. . . . I . . . I never thought of it that way. I . . . I see what you mean. It does look that way. (*Angrily.*) See now, boy? If Sheean had put it that way I'd a give him me dime. (*Hurt.*) Now, why do you suppose he didn't tell me that! Come down now. I'm sorry, sir, we've got to get out of here.

(*Music up and down.*) (*Footsteps under.*) Hurry, now, I want to get out of here. I feel terrible. I do, boy. That Sheean, that fool. Why didn't he tell me that? You'd think . . .

CHILD MONAGHAN: What does this say?

(*Footsteps halt.*)

MONAGHAN: Why, it's just a tablet, I suppose. I'll try it with me spectacles, just a minute. Why, it's a poem, I believe . . . "Give me your tired, your poor, your huddled masses yearning to breathe free, the wretched refuse of your teeming shore. Send these, the homeless, tempest-tost to me, I lift . . . my lamp beside . . . the golden door!" Oh, dear. (*Ready to weep.*) It had Welcome All on it all the time. Why didn't Sheean tell me? I'd a given him a quarter! Boy . . . go over there and here's a nickel and buy yourself a bag of them peanuts.

CHILD MONAGHAN (*astonished*): Gramp!

MONAGHAN: Go on now, I want to study this a minute. And be sure the man gives you full count.

CHILD MONAGHAN: I'll be right back.

(*Footsteps running away.*)

MONAGHAN (*to himself*): "Give me your tired, your poor, your huddled masses. . . ."

(*Music swells from a sneak to full, then under to background.*)

YOUNG MONAGHAN (*soldier*): I ran over and got my peanuts and stood there cracking them open, looking around. And I happened to glance over to grampa. He had his nose right up to that bronze tablet, reading it. And then he reached into his pocket and kinda spied around over his eyeglasses to see if anybody was

65

looking, and then he took out a coin and stuck it in a crack of the cement over the tablet. *(Coin falling onto concrete.)* It fell out and before he could pick it up I got a look at it. It was half a buck. He picked it up and pressed it into the crack so it stuck. And then he came over to me and we went home. *(Music: Change to stronger, more forceful theme.)* That's why, when I look at her now through this window, I remember that time and that poem, and she really seems to say, Whoever you are, wherever you come from, Welcome All. Welcome Home.

(Music: Flare up to finish.)

excerpt from

The Spider Plant

•

Yetta Speevack

So Long Chelsea

Twelve-year-old Carmen Santos, her older brother Pedro, and their parents have recently moved from Puerto Rico to the Chelsea section of New York City. Just as Carmen is settling happily into her new life in America, the Santos family receives word that the apartment building they live in is about to be torn down. Once again, the family will be moving. Carmen is very unhappy at the thought of leaving Chelsea.

That month going to and from school, Carmen saw many moving vans loading the furniture of families that were getting out of Chelsea. There had been moving and tearing down before, and Carmen and her friends had often stood and watched on their way home from school. But nothing like this. It was as if the whole neighborhood was suddenly torn up—as if everything had been waiting for the Santos family to decide to move. As soon as a building became vacant, a wrecking crew came to pull it down.

Sometimes one wall was left standing when it was up against a building that had not yet been emptied. By looking at such a wall, Carmen knew what colors the people had had in their apartments. One building had a green wall where the first floor had been, a blue wall for the second floor apartment and a pink one for the third floor. Between the floors a wide, dark line showed where the floor had been.

Each day the pile of old bricks where a house was coming down got larger. The wrecking crew kept fires going in the lots, burning old wood panels, floors, mattresses, chairs, and the rubbish people had discarded when they moved.

Around the vacant lots men put up fences made from the doors of vacated apartments. Like many-colored strings of beads, the fences were pink, blue, green, white, and yellow.

"I'm glad we're moving," said Papá. "It seems almost dangerous to walk the streets—bricks falling, dust flying, fires burning everywhere."

"I'm glad, too," said Mamá. "It's not pleasant to live in a house that's half empty. In the grocery store today, a woman was saying that the hot water is shut off in her building, and the building superintendent has moved out, and the man that is supposed to be the janitor never comes so the garbage never gets taken away. That could happen here, too."

"At the end of the week, I'm losing my job," said Pedro. "With people moving, Mr. Rocano's business is bad."

"Your job! That's all that matters. Don't you mind losing your friends?" asked Carmen.

"Mind your own business! That's what they say in New York," answered Pedro.

Carmen was the only one in the family who was still unhappy about moving. The thought of leaving Iris and the girls at school made her gloomy. Walking home from school was such fun. And the garden club was so exciting.

While Carmen was still wondering how she could ever leave, suddenly it was the last week. On Monday afternoon Julia had to buy a book of stamps for her mother, so the group went to the big post office and played tag on the wide steps. It was the last time she would do that, Carmen knew.

Running up and down the stairs, you had to be fast to tag somebody. When Carmen was "it" she tripped and rolled down. Her ankle hurt, but she tried not to show that she was in pain. She wanted the game to go on. "You're a good sport, Carmen," Julia said. And Carmen wondered if there would be someone to say that in the new neighborhood.

On Wednesday, Carmen and her friends watched a long crane swing a huge steel ball into a vacant building. Hundreds of bricks toppled down each time the ball smacked the building. When the steel ball struck the house, the girls shouted, "Timber," just as lumbermen do when they fell a tree in the forest.

"Let's see who can hit the house at the same time the crane does," said Mary, picking up a brick. Some of the other children picked up bricks, too, and got ready to throw. "What's the matter with the rest of you? You, Carmen, are you chicken?" Mary asked.

Remembering that she would be leaving all this fun at the end of the week, Carmen got mad, picked up a brick, and hurled it at the house with all her might.

"Get out of here," an angry workman called, chasing them. The foreman also called over, "If I catch you kids here again, I'll call the principal of your school."

Carmen ran home with the others, but she still had the urge to throw bricks.

Thursday night Carmen's family had to finish packing its belongings. Pots and pans peeked out of cartons. Sheets and pillowcases were carefully folded between tissue paper and put into the straw baskets brought from Puerto Rico.

Carmen and Pedro wrapped the dishes in newspaper and placed them in barrels the moving men had provided. Mamá had been saving newspapers since the day Papá had decided to take the apartment uptown.

Emptying drawers, shelves, and closets, Papá reminded Mamá to throw away as many old things as possible. Holding up their old meat grinder, he said, "This has done enough turns. Let's retire it."

Of a huge pot Mamá took from the closet, he said, "Did you expect to open up a restaurant in New York? Give it to somebody with a big family." Examining the kitchen chairs, which he had gotten in a secondhand shop, Papá announced, "These will keep the fire going in the lot." Next he found the hurricane lamps Mamá had brought from Puerto Rico, and he asked her, "Did you think New York had no electricity?"

Pedro and Carmen smiled at Papá's good humor. He was looking forward to a better home.

"Come, Carmen," Papá called, "hold this bundle for me while I tie a string around the things we don't need."

In a corner of the living room, he had piled the big pot, the vegetable grater, two lamps, some old picture frames, and straw baskets stuffed with old curtains.

As soon as Papá went into the kitchen to get string for the bundle, Mamá quickly removed the old pot, the picture frames, and the baskets and put them on the pile that was being moved to the new apartment. It seemed like a game to Carmen and Pedro. Papá wanted to get rid of all the old things, and Mamá wanted to save as much as she could.

Papá, on returning, noticed that some of the old things were missing from the throw-away pile.

"Please, Mamá, we are moving into a new apartment; let's buy new things."

Mamá then gave reasons for keeping the pot, the meat grinder, and other things. When Papá was not convinced, her last plea was always, "Why, I brought these things all the way from Puerto Rico."

In the end, Mamá won the game most often.

Finally it was time for Carmen to pack her personal belongings. Her first thought was for the safety of the spider plants. Transferring them to the top of the barrel of dishes, she could still hardly believe that tomorrow was her last day in Chelsea. Looking at the big spider plant, she whispered, "You didn't want to leave the sugar bowl. I had to tap you three times until you moved. Now you look bigger and better. Will it be that way with me?"

Suddenly Carmen got an idea, ran to her piggy bank, took out some money, and called to her mother as she was halfway out of the door.

"Be back soon." Before her mother could question her, Carmen was down the three flights of stairs.

She called for Iris, and together they went to the five-and-ten-cent store to buy a bag of soil. Coming back to Carmen's apartment, Iris helped her pot three spider plants in small juice cans.

Selecting the prettiest, Carmen presented the plant to Iris, saying, "It's for you, my first and best friend in Chelsea. Will you remember me?"

"Gosh, thanks, Carmen. I'll miss you. I'll write you as soon as I know where we're moving. My mother can't make up her mind between the Bronx and Brooklyn."

"I hope you move uptown, too. Write me."

Iris went home, and Carmen took one of the two remaining plants across the hall to Mrs. Morales. Mrs. Morales thanked Carmen and promised to teach María to water it.

"María will miss you," Mrs. Morales added.

"I'll miss the baby," answered Carmen.

And then it was Friday, Carmen's last day in the Chelsea school. Sometime in the morning Mamá planned to come to pick up the transfers and call for Carmen and Pedro. To her room Carmen took all her books, the little plant she had potted, and a conch shell she had brought from Puerto Rico.

"Please give this plant to somebody in the class. The shoot you gave me is big and blossoming," Carmen said softly to Miss Hall.

"Thank you, Carmen. Somebody will be glad to get this. If it is as well cared for as yours, it'll win a prize in June."

Carmen, pleased at what Miss Hall said, went back to her seat to clean out her desk. She tore up her old papers and threw them into the basket. Her crayons, scissors, and paste, she put into her book bag. She pushed the chair under her desk and brought her set of books over to Miss Hall's desk to be checked. When all the paper covers had been removed, the teacher asked her to put the books into the closet.

The class was busy copying the homework assignment for Monday when the office monitor came for Carmen's records. Miss Hall got them out of the gray box at the front of the room and gave them to the girl.

"They'll be sending for you in a few moments," Miss Hall said sadly to Carmen. As if on command, the whole class put down their pencils and looked up.

Carmen brought the conch shell to the desk, and said, "I found this on Luquillo Beach in Puerto Rico. Would you add this to your shell collection?"

"Why Carmen, this is a lovely shell with unusual markings. I've heard that Luquillo Beach is one of the most beautiful beaches in Puerto Rico. Is that true?"

Carmen and many of the children nodded their heads in agreement.

"Thank you for the shell. We'll miss you."

"Good-by, Miss Hall," said Carmen. "I'll miss you and the plants on the window sills. I still remember how you said *bienvenido* when I first came."

"Now I'll say 'Good-by and Good Luck,' " said Miss Hall. "Your next teacher is lucky to get you."

Then she nodded to Iris, who took a package from her desk and walked to the front of the room.

"Miss Hall and the class want you to have this garden book to remember us by," Iris said, handing Carmen the package.

"For me? A garden book?" Carmen was so surprised she couldn't say anything more. She just stood there holding the package. But when the monitor came to tell Miss Hall that Carmen's mother was waiting, Iris urged, "Open it, Carmen."

She opened it then and couldn't hold back the tears as she did. So she waved good-by and started out with the monitor for the office.

"Good-by, good-by." The sound followed her down the hall. And then there was another call:

"Carmen, Carmen." It was Iris. "*Mira*, look, your book bag."

"Write me, Iris. Write me about the class," begged Carmen.

"*Si*," said her first New York friend, still talking Spanish as she had had to do the first day they met.

"Talk English in school," said the monitor, who wanted to know what they were saying.

This remark made Carmen angry; she brushed back her tears and said, "We'll talk whatever we please."

She and Iris laughed, and Iris said "Good-by" and ran back to her class.

When Carmen got down to the office, Mamá and Pedro were already waiting. The clerk gave them an envelope, and they started for home. Pedro questioned Mamá about the moving men, but Carmen walked behind slowly without speaking.

"Let's walk faster," said Mamá. "We still have things to do."

"Mamá," said Carmen, "do you remember the houses on this street when we first moved to Chelsea? Some were small and others so tall I had to bend my head back to see the top floor. Now they will build even taller buildings, with grass and trees between. But I'll always remember the old and poor houses that were here when we first came. People were happy in them because I heard singing from inside."

"A neighborhood has to be cleaned up," said Mamá.

"Often I felt like singing myself because there were good people in Chelsea," Carmen continued.

"Stop being unhappy," said Mamá. "There are good people everywhere."

Carmen walked faster, but she kept looking around and saying very softly, "So long. So long, Chelsea."

WORMS AND THE WIND

Carl Sandburg

Worms would rather be worms.
Ask a worm and he says, 'Who knows what a worm
knows?'
Worms go down and up and over and under.
Worms like tunnels.
When worms talk they talk about the worm world.
Worms like it in the dark.
Neither the sun nor the moon interests a worm.

Zigzag worms hate circle worms.
Curve worms never trust square worms.
Worms know what worms want.
Slide worms are suspicious of crawl worms.
One worm asks another, 'How does your belly drag today?'
The shape of a crooked worm satisfies a crooked worm.
A straight worm says, 'Why not be straight?'
Worms tired of crawling begin to slither.
Long worms slither farther than short worms.
Middle-sized worms say, 'It is nice to be neither long nor short.'
Old worms teach young worms to say, 'Don't be sorry for me unless you have been a worm and lived in worm places and read worm books.'
When worms go to war they dig in, come out and fight, dig in again, come out and fight again, dig in again, and so on.
Worms underground never hear the wind overground and sometimes they ask, 'What is this wind we hear of?'

excerpt from

Charlotte's Web

E. B. White
illustrated by Garth Williams

Before Breakfast

The book Charlotte's Web *tells the story of the friendship between a girl named Fern, her pet pig Wilbur, and a spider named Charlotte.*

"Where's Papa going with that ax?" said Fern to her mother as they were setting the table for breakfast. "Out to the hoghouse," replied Mrs. Arable. "Some pigs were born last night."

"I don't see why he needs an ax," continued Fern, who was only eight.

"Well," said her mother, "one of the pigs is a runt. It's very small and weak, and it will never amount to anything. So your father has decided to do away with it."

"Do *away* with it?" shrieked Fern. "You mean *kill* it? Just because it's smaller than the others?"

Mrs. Arable put a pitcher of cream on the table. "Don't yell, Fern!" she said. "Your father is right. The pig would probably die anyway."

Fern pushed a chair out of the way and ran outdoors. The grass was wet and the earth smelled of springtime. Fern's sneakers were sopping by the time she caught up with her father.

"Please don't kill it!" she sobbed. "It's unfair."

Mr. Arable stopped walking.

"Fern," he said gently, "you will have to learn to control yourself."

"Control myself?" yelled Fern. "This is a matter of life and death, and you talk about *controlling* myself." Tears ran down her cheeks and she took hold of the ax and tried to pull it out of her father's hand.

"Fern," said Mr. Arable, "I know more about raising a litter of pigs than you do. A weakling makes trouble. Now run along!"

"But it's unfair," cried Fern. "The pig couldn't help being born small, could it? If *I* had been very small at birth, would you have killed *me*?"

Mr. Arable smiled. "Certainly not," he said, looking down at his daughter with love. "But this is different. A little girl is one thing, a little runty pig is another."

"I see no difference," replied Fern, still hanging on to the ax. "This is the most terrible case of injustice I ever heard of."

A queer look came over John Arable's face. He seemed almost ready to cry himself.

"All right," he said. "You go back to the house and I will bring the runt when I come in. I'll let you start it on a bottle, like a baby. Then you'll see what trouble a pig can be."

When Mr. Arable returned to the house half an hour later, he carried a carton under his arm. Fern was upstairs changing her sneakers. The kitchen table was set for breakfast, and the room smelled of coffee, bacon, damp plaster, and wood smoke from the stove.

"Put it on her chair!" said Mrs. Arable. Mr. Arable set the carton down at Fern's place. Then he walked to the sink and washed his hands and dried them on the roller towel.

Fern came slowly down the stairs. Her eyes were red from crying. As she approached her chair, the carton wobbled, and there was a scratching noise. Fern looked at her father. Then she lifted the lid of the carton. There, inside, looking up at her, was the newborn pig. It was a white one. The morning light shone through its ears, turning them pink.

"He's yours," said Mr. Arable. "Saved from an untimely death. And may the good Lord forgive me for this foolishness."

Fern couldn't take her eyes off the tiny pig. "Oh," she
whispered. "Oh, *look* at him! He's absolutely perfect."

She closed the carton carefully. First she kissed her
father, then she kissed her mother. Then she opened the
lid again, lifted the pig out, and held it against her cheek.
At this moment her brother Avery came into the room.
Avery was ten. He was heavily armed—an air rifle in one
hand, a wooden dagger in the other.

"What's that?" he demanded. "What's Fern got?"

"She's got a guest for breakfast," said Mrs. Arable.
"Wash your hands and face, Avery!"

"Let's see it!" said Avery, setting his gun down. "You
call that miserable thing a pig? That's a *fine* specimen of a
pig—it's no bigger than a white rat."

"Wash up and eat your breakfast, Avery!" said his
mother. "The school bus will be along in half an hour."

"Can I have a pig, too, Pop?" asked Avery.

"No, I only distribute pigs to early risers," said Mr. Arable. "Fern was up at daylight, trying to rid the world of injustice. As a result, she now has a pig. A small one, to be sure, but nevertheless a pig. It just shows what can happen if a person gets out of bed promptly. Let's eat!"

But Fern couldn't eat until her pig had had a drink of milk. Mrs. Arable found a baby's nursing bottle and a rubber nipple. She poured warm milk into the bottle, fitted the nipple over the top, and handed it to Fern. "Give him his breakfast!" she said.

A minute later, Fern was seated on the floor in the corner of the kitchen with her infant between her knees, teaching it to suck from the bottle. The pig, although tiny, had a good appetite and caught on quickly.

The school bus honked from the road.

"Run!" commanded Mrs. Arable, taking the pig from Fern and slipping a doughnut into her hand. Avery grabbed his gun and another doughnut.

The children ran out to the road and climbed into the bus. Fern took no notice of the others in the bus. She just sat and stared out of the window, thinking what a blissful world it was and how lucky she was to have entire charge of a pig. By the time the bus reached school, Fern had named her pet, selecting the most beautiful name she could think of.

"Its name is Wilbur," she whispered to herself.

She was still thinking about the pig when the teacher said: "Fern, what is the capital of Pennsylvania?"

"Wilbur," replied Fern, dreamily. The pupils giggled. Fern blushed.

Afternoon
Robert Sund

with just enough of a breeze for him to ride it
lazily, a hawk
sails still-winged
up the slope of a stubble-covered hill,
so low
he nearly
touches his shadow.

Raymond's Run

Toni Cade Bambara

I don't have much work to do around the house like some girls. My mother does that. And I don't have to earn my pocket money by hustling; George runs errands for the big boys and sells Christmas cards. And anything else that's got to get done, my father does. All I have to do in life is mind my brother Raymond, which is enough.

Sometimes I slip and say my little brother Raymond. But as any fool can see he's much bigger and he's older too. But a lot of people call him my little brother cause he needs looking after cause he's not quite right. And a lot of smart mouths got lots to say about that too, especially when George was minding him. But now, if anybody has anything to say to Raymond, anything to say about his big head, they have to come to me. And I don't play the dozens or believe in standing around with somebody in my face doing a lot of talking. I much rather just knock you down and take my chances even if I am a little girl with skinny arms and a squeaky voice, which is how I got the name Squeaky. And if things get too rough, I run. And as anybody can tell you, I'm the fastest thing on two feet.

There is no track meet that I don't win the first place medal. I used to win the twenty-yard dash when I was a little kid in kindergarten. Nowadays, it's the fifty-yard dash. And tomorrow I'm subject to run the quarter-meter relay all by myself and come in first, second, and third. The big kids call me Mercury cause I'm the swiftest thing in the neighborhood. Everybody knows that—except two

people who know better, my father and me. He can beat me to Amsterdam Avenue with me having a two fire-hydrant headstart and him running with his hands in his pockets and whistling. But that's private information. Cause can you imagine some thirty-five-year-old man stuffing himself into PAL shorts to race little kids? So as far as everyone's concerned, I'm the fastest and that goes for Gretchen, too, who has put out the tale that she is going to win the first-place medal this year. Ridiculous. In the second place, she's got short legs. In the third place, she's got freckles. In the first place, no one can beat me and that's all there is to it.

I'm standing on the corner admiring the weather and about to take a stroll down Broadway so I can practice my breathing exercises, and I've got Raymond walking on the inside close to the buildings, cause he's subject to fits of fantasy and starts thinking he's a circus performer and that the curb is a tightrope strung high in the air. And sometimes after a rain he likes to step down off his tightrope right into the gutter and slosh around getting his shoes and cuffs wet. Then I get hit when I get home. Or sometimes if you don't watch him he'll dash across traffic to the island in the middle of Broadway and give the pigeons a fit. Then I have to go behind him apologizing to all the old people sitting around trying to get some sun and getting all upset with the pigeons fluttering around them, scattering their newspapers and upsetting the waxpaper lunches in their laps. So I keep Raymond on the inside of me, and he plays like he's driving a stage coach which is O.K. by me so long as he doesn't run me over or interrupt my breathing exercises, which I have to do on account of I'm serious about my running and don't care who knows it.

Now some people like to act like things come easy to them, won't let on that they practice. Not me. I'll high-prance down 34th Street like a rodeo pony to keep my knees strong even if it does get my mother uptight so that she walks ahead like she's not with me, don't know me, is all by herself on a shopping trip, and I am somebody else's crazy child. Now you take Cynthia Procter for instance. She's just the opposite. If there's a test tomorrow, she'll

84

say something like, "Oh, I guess I'll play handball this afternoon and watch television tonight," just to let you know she ain't thinking about the test. Or like last week when she won the spelling bee for the millionth time, "A good thing you got 'receive,' Squeaky, cause I would have got it wrong. I completely forgot about the spelling bee." And she'll clutch the lace on her blouse like it was a narrow escape. Oh, brother. But of course when I pass her house on my early morning trots around the block, she is practicing the scales on the piano over and over and over and over. Then in music class she always lets herself get bumped around so she falls accidently on purpose onto the piano stool and is so surprised to find herself sitting there that she decides just for fun to try out the ole keys. And what do you know—Chopin's waltzes just spring out of her fingertips and she's the most surprised thing in the world. A regular prodigy. I could kill people like that. I stay up all night studying the words for the spelling bee. And you can see me anytime of day practicing running. I never walk if I can trot, and shame on Raymond if he can't keep up. But of course he does, cause if he hangs back someone's liable to walk up to him and get smart, or take his allowance from him, or ask him where he got that great big pumpkin head. People are so stupid sometimes.

So I'm strolling down Broadway breathing out and breathing in on counts of seven, which is my lucky number, and here comes Gretchen and her sidekicks: Mary Louise, who used to be a friend of mine when she first moved to Harlem from Baltimore and got beat up by everybody till I took up for her on account of her mother and my mother used to sing in the same choir when they were young girls, but people ain't grateful, so now she hangs out with the new girl Gretchen and talks about me like a dog; and Rosie, who is as fat as I am skinny and has a big mouth where Raymond is concerned and is too stupid to know that there is not a big deal of difference between herself and Raymond and that she can't afford to throw stones. So they are steady coming up Broadway and I see right away that it's going to be one of those Dodge City scenes cause the street ain't that big and they're close to the buildings just as we are. First I think I'll step into the candy store and look over the new comics and let them pass. But that's chicken and I've got a reputation to consider. So then I think I'll just walk straight on through them or even over them if necessary. But as they get to me, they slow down. I'm ready to fight, cause like I said I don't feature a whole lot of chit-chat, I much prefer to just knock you down right from the jump and save everybody a lotta precious time.

"You signing up for the May Day races?" smiles Mary Louise, only it's not a smile at all. A dumb question like that doesn't deserve an answer. Besides, there's just me and Gretchen standing there really, so no use wasting my breath talking to shadows.

"I don't think you're going to win this time," says Rosie, trying to signify with her hands on her hips all salty, completely forgetting that I have whupped her behind many times for less salt than that.

"I always win cause I'm the best," I say straight at Gretchen who is, as far as I'm concerned, the only one talking in this ventriloquist-dummy routine. Gretchen smiles, but it's not a smile, and I'm thinking that girls never really smile at each other because they don't know how and don't want to know how and there's probably no one to teach us how, cause grown-up girls don't know either. Then they all look at Raymond who has just brought his mule team to a standstill. And they're about to see what trouble they can get into through him.

"What grade you in now, Raymond?"

"You got anything to say to my brother, you say it to me, Mary Louise Williams of Raggedy Town, Baltimore."

"What are you, his mother?" sasses Rosie.

"That's right, Fatso. And the next word out of anybody and I'll be *their* mother too." So they just stand there and Gretchen shifts from one leg to the other and so do they. Then Gretchen puts her hands on her hips and is about to say something with her freckle-face self but doesn't. Then she walks around me looking me up and down but keeps walking up Broadway, and her sidekicks follow her. So me and Raymond smile at each other and he says, "Gidyap" to his team and I continue with my breathing exercises, strolling down Broadway toward the ice man on 145th with not a care in the world cause I am Miss Quicksilver herself.

I take my time getting to the park on May Day because the track meet is the last thing on the program. The biggest thing on the program is the May Pole dancing, which I can do without, thank you, even if my mother thinks it's a shame I don't take part and act like a girl for a change. You'd think my mother'd be grateful not to have to make me a white organdy dress with a big satin sash and buy me new white baby-doll shoes that can't be taken out of the box till the big day. You'd think she'd be glad her daughter ain't out there prancing around a May Pole getting the new clothes all dirty and sweaty and trying to act like a fairy or a flower or whatever you're supposed to be when you should be trying to be yourself, whatever that is, which is, as far as I am concerned, a poor Black girl who really can't afford to buy shoes and a new dress you only wear once a lifetime cause it won't fit next year.

I was once a strawberry in a Hansel and Gretel pageant when I was in nursery school and didn't have no better sense than to dance on tiptoe with my arms in a circle over my head doing umbrella steps and being a perfect fool just so my mother and father could come dressed up and clap. You'd think they'd know better than to encourage that kind of nonsense. I am not a strawberry. I do not dance on my toes. I run. That is what I am all about. So I always come late to the May Day program, just in time to get my number pinned on and lay in the grass till they announce the fifty-yard dash.

I put Raymond in the little swings, which is a tight squeeze this year and will be impossible next year. Then I look around for Mr. Pearson, who pins the numbers on. I'm really looking for Gretchen if you want to know the truth, but she's not around. The park is jam-packed. Parents in hats and corsages and breast-pocket handkerchiefs peeking up. Kids in white dresses and light-blue suits. The parkees unfolding chairs and chasing the rowdy kids from Lenox as if they had no right to be there. The big guys with their caps on backwards, leaning against the fence swirling the basketballs on the tips of their fingers, waiting for all these crazy people to clear out the park so they can play. Most of the kids in my class are carrying bass drums and glockenspiels and flutes. You'd think they'd put in a few bongos or something for real like that.

Then here comes Mr. Pearson with his clipboard and his cards and pencils and whistles and safety pins and fifty million other things he's always dropping all over the place with his clumsy self. He sticks out in a crowd cause he's on stilts. We used to call him Jack and the Beanstalk to get him mad. But I'm the only one that can outrun him and get away, and I'm too grown for that silliness now.

"Well, Squeaky," he says, checking my name off the list and handing me number seven and two pins. And I'm thinking he's got no right to call me Squeaky, if I can't call him Beanstalk.

"Hazel Elizabeth Deborah Parker," I correct him and tell him to write it down on his board.

"Well, Hazel Elizabeth Deborah Parker, going to give someone else a break this year?" I squint at him real hard to see if he is seriously thinking I should lose the race on purpose just to give someone else a break. "Only six girls running this time," he continues, shaking his head sadly like it's my fault all of New York didn't turn out in sneakers. "That new girl should give you a run for your money." He looks around the park for Gretchen like a periscope in a submarine movie. "Wouldn't it be a nice gesture if you were . . . to ahhh . . ."

I give him such a look he couldn't finish putting that idea into words. Grownups got a lot of nerve sometimes. I pin number seven to myself and stomp away, I'm so burnt. And I go straight for the track and stretch out on the grass while the band winds up with "Oh, the Monkey Wrapped His Tail Around the Flag Pole," which my teacher calls by some other name. The man on the loudspeaker is calling everyone over to the track and I'm on my back looking at the sky, trying to pretend I'm in the country, but I can't, because even grass in the city feels hard as sidewalk, and there's just no pretending you are anywhere but in a "concrete jungle" as my grandfather says.

The twenty-yard dash takes all of two minutes cause most of the kids don't know no better than to run off the

track or run the wrong way or run smack into the fence and fall down and cry. One little kid, though, has got the good sense to run straight for the white ribbon up ahead so he wins. Then the second-graders line up for the thirty-yard dash and I don't even bother to turn my head to watch cause Raphael Perez always wins. He wins before he even begins by psyching the runners, telling them they're going to trip on their shoelaces and fall on their faces or lose their shorts or something, which he doesn't really have to do since he is very fast, almost as fast as I am. After that is the forty-yard dash which I use to run when I was in first grade. Raymond is hollering from the swings cause he knows I'm about to do my thing cause the man on the loudspeaker has just announced the fifty-yard dash, although he might just as well be giving a recipe for angel food cake cause you can hardly make out what he's sayin for the static. I get up and slip off my sweat pants and then I see Gretchen standing at the starting line, kicking her legs out like a pro. Then as I get into place I see that ole Raymond is on line on the other side of the fence, bending down with his fingers on the ground just like he knew what he was doing. I was going to yell at him but then I didn't. It burns up your energy to holler.

Every time, just before I take off in a race, I always feel like I'm in a dream, the kind of dream you have when you're sick with fever and feel all hot and weightless. I dream I'm flying over a sandy beach in the early morning sun, kissing the leaves of the trees as I fly by. And there's always the smell of apples, just like in the country when I was little and used to think I was a choo-choo train, running through the fields of corn and chugging up the hill to the orchard. And all the time I'm dreaming this, I get lighter and lighter until I'm flying over the beach again, getting blown through the sky like a feather that weighs nothing at all. But once I spread my fingers in the dirt and crouch over the Get on Your Mark, the dream goes and I am solid again and am telling myself, Squeaky you must win, you must win, you are the fastest thing in the world, you can even beat your father up Amsterdam if you really try. And then I feel my weight coming back just behind my knees then down to my feet then into the earth and

90

the pistol shot explodes in my blood and I am off and weightless again, flying past the other runners, my arms pumping up and down and the whole world is quiet except for the crunch as I zoom over the gravel in the track. I glance to my left and there is no one. To the right, a blurred Gretchen, who's got her chin jutting out as if it would win the race all by itself. And on the other side of the fence is Raymond with his arms down to his side and the palms tucked up behind him, running in his very own style, and it's the first time I ever saw that and I almost stop to watch my brother Raymond on his first run. But the white ribbon is bouncing toward me and I tear past it, racing into the distance till my feet with a mind of their own start digging up footfuls of dirt and brake me short. Then all the kids standing on the side pile on me, banging me on the back and slapping my head with their May Day programs, for I have won again and everybody on 151st Street can walk tall for another year.

"In first place . . ." the man on the loudspeaker is clear as a bell now. But then he pauses and the loudspeaker starts to whine. Then static. And I lean down to catch my breath and here comes Gretchen walking back, for she's overshot the finish line too, huffing and puffing with her hands on her hips taking it slow, breathing in steady time like a real pro and I sort of like her a little for the first time. "In first place . . ." and then three or four voices get all mixed up on the loudspeaker and I dig my sneaker into the grass and stare at Gretchen who's staring

91

back, we both wondering just who did win. I can hear old Beanstalk arguing with the man on the loudspeaker and then a few others running their mouths about what the stopwatches say. Then I hear Raymond yanking at the fence to call me and I wave to shush him, but he keeps rattling the fence like a gorilla in a cage like in them gorilla movies, but then like a dancer or something he starts climbing up nice and easy but very fast. And it occurs to me, watching how smoothly he climbs hand over hand and remembering how he looked running with his arms down to his side and with the wind pulling his mouth back and his teeth showing and all, it occurred to me that Raymond would make a very fine runner. Doesn't he always keep up with me on my trots? And he surely knows how to breathe in counts of seven cause he's always doing it at the dinner table, which drives my brother George up the wall. And I'm smiling to beat the band cause if I've lost this race, or if me and Gretchen tied, or even if I've won, I can always retire as a runner and begin a whole new career as a coach with Raymond as my champion. After all, with a little more study I can beat Cynthia and her phony self at the spelling bee. And if I bugged my mother, I could get piano lessons and become a star. And I have a big rep as the baddest thing around. And I've got a roomful of ribbons and medals and awards. But what has Raymond got to call his own?

So I stand there with my new plan, laughing out loud by this time as Raymond jumps down from the fence and runs over with his teeth showing and his arms down to the side, which no one before him has quite mastered as a running style. And by the time he comes over I'm jumping up and down so glad to see him—my brother Raymond, a great runner in the family tradition. But of course everyone thinks I'm jumping up and down because the men on the loudspeaker have finally gotten themselves together and compared notes and are announcing "In first place—Miss Hazel Elizabeth Deborah Parker." (Dig that.) "In second place—Miss Gretchen P. Lewis." And I look over at Gretchen wondering what the "P" stands for. And I smile. Cause she's good, no doubt about it. Maybe she'd like to help me coach Raymond; she obviously is serious about running, as any fool can see. And she nods to congratulate me and then she smiles. And I smile. We stand there with this big smile of respect between us. It's about as real a smile as girls can do for each other, considering we don't practice real smiling every day, you know, cause maybe we too busy being flowers or fairies or strawberries instead of something honest and worthy of respect . . . you know . . . like being people.

Madness One Monday Evening
Julia Fields

Late that mad Monday evening
I made mermaids come from the sea
As the black sky sat
Upon the waves
And night came
Creeping up to me

    (I tell you I made mermaids
    Come from the sea)

The green waves lulled and rolled
As I sat by the locust tree
And the bright glare of the neon world
Sent gas-words bursting free—
Their spewed splendor fell on the billows
And gaudy it grew to me
As I sat up upon the shore
And made mermaids come from the sea.

excerpt from

The Black Stallion

Walter Farley

*T*he Black Stallion *tells the exciting story of
friendship between a boy and "the wildest of all wild
creatures"—a wild stallion. The boy, Alec, and the horse
("the Black") meet on board ship, where Alec tries to befriend
the horse by feeding him sugar. When the ship sinks,
the horse pulls Alec to the safety of
a small island.*

The Island

Alec opened his eyes. The sun, high in the heavens, beat down upon his bare head. His face felt hot, his tongue swollen. Slowly he pushed his tired body from the ground and then fell back upon the sand. He lay still a few moments. Then he gathered himself and once again attempted to rise. Wearily he got to his knees, then to his feet. His legs trembled beneath him. He unbuckled the battered life jacket and let it fall to the ground.

He looked around; he needed water desperately. He saw the Black's hoof marks in the sand. Perhaps, if he followed them, they would lead him to fresh water; he was sure that the stallion was as thirsty as he. Alec stumbled along. The hoof marks turned abruptly away from the ocean toward the interior of the island. There was no sign of vegetation around him—only hot sand. He turned and looked back at the now calm and peaceful sea. So much had happened in such a short space of time! What had happened to the others? Was he the only one who had survived?

A few minutes later he turned and made his way up a high sand dune. At the crest he stopped. From where he stood he could see the entire island; it was small—not more than two miles in circumference. It seemed barren except for a few trees, bushes and scattered patches of burned grass. High rock cliffs dropped down to the sea on the other side of the island.

The Black's hoof marks led down the hill, and a short distance away beneath a few scattered trees, Alec saw a small spring-water pool. His swollen tongue ran across cracked lips as he stumbled forward. To the right of the spring, a hundred yards away, he saw the Black—hungrily feasting upon the dry grass. Alec again saw that small Arabian port and the crowd gathered around the prone figure of the Arab whom the Black had struck. Would he be safe from the stallion?

The Black looked up from his grazing. The boy noticed that the horse had torn or slipped off his halter somehow.

The wind whipped through his mane; his smooth black body was brilliant in the sun. He saw Alec, and his shrill whistle echoed through the air. He reared, his front legs striking out. Then he came down, and his right foreleg pawed into the dirt.

Alec looked around him. There was no place to seek cover. He was too weak to run, even if there was. His gaze returned to the stallion, fascinated by a creature so wild and so near. Here was the wildest of all wild animals—he had fought for everything he had ever needed, for food, for leadership, for life itself; it was his nature to kill or be killed. The horse reared again; then he snorted and plunged straight for the boy.

Alec didn't move. His body was numb. Hypnotized, he watched the stallion coming. Then, twenty-five yards from him, the Black stopped. The whites of his eyes gleamed, his nostrils curled, his ears were back flat against his head. He whistled shrill, clear and long. Suddenly he moved between Alec and the spring. He pawed furiously at the earth.

Alec stood still, not daring to move. After what seemed hours, the stallion stopped tearing up the earth. His gaze turned from the boy to the pool and then back again. He whistled, half-reared, and then broke into his long stride, running back in the direction from which he had come.

Alec forced his legs into action, reached the spring and threw himself on the ground beside it. He let his face fall into the cool, clear water. It seemed that he would never get enough; he doused his head, and let the water run down his back. Then he tore off part of his shirt and bathed his skinned body. Refreshed, he crawled beneath the shaded bushes growing beside the pool. He stretched out, closed his eyes and fell asleep, exhausted.

Only once during the night did Alec stir; sleepily he opened his eyes. He could see the moon through the bushes, high above the star-studded sky. A big, black figure moved by the spring—the Black, and only a few feet away! He drank deeply and then raised his beautiful head, his ears pricked forward; he turned and trotted away.

Alec awoke very hungry the next morning. He had gone a day and a half without eating! He rose and drank from the spring. The next thing was to find food. He walked for quite some distance before he found anything edible. It was a berry bush; the fruit was unlike that of anything he had ever tasted before. But he might not easily find anything else that he could eat, so he made a meal of berries.

Then he explored the island. He found it to be flat between the sand dune that he had climbed the day before and the rocky cliffs of the other side of the island. He made no attempt to climb over the large boulders. There were few berry bushes and little grass, and Alec realized that food would be scarce for him and the Black. The island seemed to be totally uninhabited. He had seen no birds or animals of any kind.

He walked slowly back in the direction of the spring. From the top of the hill he looked out upon the open sea, hoping desperately that he would see a boat. Only the vast expanse of blue water spread before him. Below he saw the Black cantering along the beach. Alec forgot his problems in the beauty of the stallion as he swept along, graceful in his swift stride, his black mane and tail flying. When the horse vanished around the bend of the island, Alec walked down to the beach.

The next thing that he must do was to erect some sort of a shelter for himself; and first he must find driftwood. Alec's eyes swept the shore. He saw one piece, then another.

For the next few hours he struggled with the wood that he found cast upon the beach, dragging it back toward the spring. He piled it up and was surprised to see how much he had gathered. He looked for a long, heavy piece and found one that suited his purpose. He pulled it toward two adjoining scrub trees and hoisted it between the two crotches. Suddenly his arms shook and he stopped. Painted on the gray board was the name DRAKE—it had been part of one of the lifeboats! Alec stood still a moment, then grimly he fixed the plank securely in place.

Next he leaned the remaining pieces of wood on each side of the plank, making a shelter in the form of a tent.

99

He filled in the open ends as well as he could. With his knife he skinned the bark from a tree and tied the pieces of wood together.

Alec went back to the beach and gathered all the seaweed that he could carry. He stuffed this into all the open holes. He surveyed his finished shelter—he was afraid a good wind would blow it down on top of him!

He looked up at the hot sun and guessed it to be near noon. His skin and clothes were wet with perspiration from the terrific heat. He cut a long, slender staff from a tree, tested it and found it to be strong. Carefully he skinned it and cut it the right length. Then he tied his knife securely to the end of the stick with a piece of bark.

A short time later Alec stood beside a small cove which he had discovered that morning. The water was clear and the sand glistened white beneath it. He seated himself upon the bank and peered eagerly into the water. He had read of people catching fish this way. After some time he saw a ripple. Carefully he raised his improvised spear. Then Alec flung it with all his might; the long stick whizzed down into the water and pierced its way into the white sand. He had missed!

He pulled his spear out and moved to another spot. Again he waited patiently. It was a long time before he saw another fish. A long slender shape moved in the shallow water beneath him. He raised his spear, took aim and plunged again. He saw the knife hit! Fearing the knife would slip out of the fish if he pulled the spear up, he jumped into the shallow water and shoved it against the bottom. Desperately Alec's arm flew down the stick, seeking the fish. The water was churned with sand. He came to the end, only the steel blade met his searching fingers. He had lost it!

For the rest of the afternoon, Alec strove to catch a fish. As darkness fell, he rose wearily to his feet and walked slowly back to his new "home." His eyes ached from the hours of strain of constant searching into the depths of the water.

On his way, he stopped at the berry bush and ate hungrily. When he reached the spring, he saw the Black not far away. He looked up, saw the boy and continued to eat. Moving from one place to another, he tore away at the small patches of grass that he could find. "I'll bet he's as hungry as I am," thought Alec. He dropped down and drank from the spring.

Darkness came rapidly. Suddenly Alec felt the stillness of the island—no birds, no animals, no sounds. It was as if he and the Black were the only living creatures in the world. Millions of stars shone overhead and seemed so close. The moon rose high and round; its reflection cast upon the pool.

The Black looked up from his grazing. He, too, seemed to watch the moon. Alec whistled—low, then louder and fading. A moment of silence. Then the stallion's shrill whistle pierced the night. Alec saw the Black look in his direction and then continue searching for grass. He smiled and crawled into his shelter. The day's work had made him tired and he was soon asleep.

The next morning found Alec beside the cove again with his spear, determined to catch a fish for breakfast. At noon he ate berries. Mid-afternoon he was sick; his head whirled and he could hardly keep his eyes from closing.

A small whirlpool appeared on the surface of the water. Alec grabbed the spear beside him and rose to his knees. He saw a gray shape in the water below. He raised his spear and moved it along with the fish. Then he plunged it! The spear quivered in its flight. He had hit! He jumped into the water, shoving the spear and fish against the bottom. He mustn't lose this one! His hand reached the knife. The fish was there—wriggling, fighting. Then he had it. Quickly he raised the fish from the water and threw it, and the spear, onto the bank. Wearily he climbed up and looked at his catch. "Two feet if it's an inch," he said hungrily. He drew out the spear, picked up the fish and went back to camp.

Alec washed the fish in the spring. Then he placed it upon a piece of wood and scaled it. Now if he could only get a fire started. He remembered watching a man in India build a fire without matches. Perhaps he could do the same.

He gathered some small pieces of bark, dry wood and a deserted bird's nest, and spread them on the ground in front of him. He picked out the driest piece of wood and, with his knife, bored a hole halfway through it. Carefully he tore small threads of straw from the bird's nest and placed them inside the hole; they would ignite quickly. Next he cut a sturdy elastic branch about eighteen inches long from a nearby tree, skinned it and placed one end in the hole. He leaned on the stick, bending it, and then rapidly turned the curved part like a carpenter's bit.

It seemed to Alec that an hour passed before a small column of smoke crept out of the hole. His tired arms pushed harder. Slowly a small flame grew and then the dry wood was on fire. He added more wood. Then he snatched the fish, wrapped it in some seaweed which he had previously washed, and placed it on top of the fire.

Later, Alec removed the fish. He tried a piece and found it to be good. Famished, he tore into the rest of it.

The days passed and the boy strove desperately to find food to keep himself alive; he caught only one more fish—it would be impossible for him to depend upon the sea for his living. He turned again to the berries, but they were fast diminishing. He managed to keep his fire going as the heat made dry fuel plentiful. However, that was of little use to him as he had nothing to cook.

One day as Alec walked along the beach, he saw a large red shell in the distance. He gripped his spear tighter; it looked like a turtle. Then hunger made him lose all caution and he rushed forward, his spear raised. He threw himself upon the shell, his knife digging into the opening where he believed the turtle's head to be. Desperately he turned the huge shell over—it was empty, cleaned out; only the hollow shell met Alec's famished gaze. He stood still, dazed. Then slowly he turned and walked back to camp.

The Black was drinking from the spring. His large body too was beginning to show signs of starvation. Alec no longer felt any fear of him. The stallion raised his proud head and looked at the boy. Then he turned and trotted off. His mane, long and flowing, whipped in the wind. His whistle filled the air.

Alec watched him, envying his proud, wild spirit. The horse was used to the hardships of the desert; probably he would outlive him. The boy's subconscious thought rose to the surface of his mind: "There's food, Alec, food—if you could only find some way of killing him!" Then he shook his head, hating himself. Kill the animal that had saved his life? Never—even if he could, he would die of starvation first! The stallion reached the top of the hill and stood there, like a beautiful black statue, his gaze upon the open sea.

One morning Alec made his way weakly toward the rocky side of the island. He came to the huge rocks and climbed on top of one of them. It was more barren than any other part of the island. It was low tide and Alec's eyes wandered over the stony shore, looking for any kind of shellfish he might be able to eat. He noticed the mosslike substance on all the rocks at the water's edge, and on those that extended out. What was that stuff the biology teacher had made them eat last term in one of their experiments? Hadn't he called it *carragheen?* Yes, that was it. A sort of seaweed, he had said, that grew abundantly along the rocky parts of the Atlantic coast of Europe and North America. When washed and dried, it was edible for humans and livestock. Could the moss on the rocks below be it? Alec scarcely dared to hope.

Slowly Alec made the dangerous descent. He reached the water level and scrambled across the rocks. He took a handful of the soft greenish-yellow moss which covered them and raised it to his lips. It smelled the same. He tasted it. The moss was terribly salty from the sea, but it was the same as he had eaten that day in the classroom!

Eagerly he filled his pockets with it, then removed his shirt and filled it full. He climbed up again and hurried back to camp. Then he emptied the moss onto the ground beside the spring. The next quarter of an hour he spent washing it, and then placed it out in the sun to dry. Hungrily he tasted it again. It was better—and it was food!

When he had finished eating, the sun was falling into the ocean, and the skies were rapidly growing dark. In the distance Alec saw the stallion coming toward the spring.

Quickly he picked up some of the moss for himself and left the rest on the ground beside the pool. Would the Black eat it? Alec hurried to his shelter and stood still watching intently.

The stallion rushed up, shook his long neck and buried his mouth into the water. He drank long. When he had finished he looked toward the boy, then his pink nostrils quivered. The Black put his nose to the ground and walked toward the moss which Alec had left. He sniffed at it. Then he picked a little up and started eating. He chewed long and carefully. He reached down for more.

That night Alec slept better than he had since he had been on the island. He had found food—food to sustain him and the Black!

The Wildest of All Wild Creatures

The next day Alec set out to obtain more of the carragheen. As he neared the rocks, he saw the stallion standing silently beside a huge boulder. Not a muscle twitched in his black body—it was as if an artist had painted the Black on white stone.

Alec climbed down into a small hollow and paused to look out over the rocks below. Suddenly he heard the stallion's scream, more piercing, more blood-curdling than he had ever heard it before. He looked up.

The Black was on his hind legs, his teeth bared. Then with a mighty leap, he shot away from the boulder toward Alec. Swiftly he came—faster with every magnificent stride. He was almost on top of him when he thundered to a halt and reared again. Alec jumped to the side, tripped on a stone and fell to the ground. High above him the Black's legs pawed the air, and then descended three yards in front of him! Again he went up and down—again and again he pounded. The ground on which Alec lay shook from the force of his hoofs. The stallion's eyes never left the ground in front of him.

Gradually his pounding lessened and then stopped. He raised his head high and his whistle shrilled through the air. He shook his head and slowly moved away, his nostrils trembling.

Alec regained his feet and cautiously made his way toward the torn earth, his brain flooded with confusion. There in front of him he saw the strewn parts of a long, yellowish-black body, and the venomous head of a snake, crushed and lifeless. He stood still—the suddenness of discovering life, other than the Black and himself on the island, astounding him! Sweat broke out on his forehead as he realized what a poisonous snake bite would have meant—suffering and perhaps death! Dazed, he looked at the stallion just a few feet away. Had the Black killed the snake to save him? Was the stallion beginning to understand that they needed each other to survive?

Slowly the boy walked toward the Black. The stallion's mane swept in the wind, his muscles twitched, his eyes moved restlessly, but he stood his ground as the boy approached. Alec wanted the horse to understand that he would not hurt him. Cautiously he reached a hand toward the stallion's head. The Black drew it back as far as he could without moving. Alec stepped closer and to the side of him. Gently he touched him for an instant. The stallion did not move. Again Alec attempted to touch the savage head. The Black reared and shook a little. Alec said soothingly, "Steady, Black fellow, I wouldn't hurt you." The stallion quivered, then reared again and broke. One hundred yards away he suddenly stopped and turned.

Alec gazed at him, standing there so still—his head raised high in the air. "We'll get out of this somehow, Black—working together," he said determinedly.

Alec walked back to the top of the rocks and again began his descent. He made his way carefully down to the water level. Cautiously he looked before he stepped— where there was one snake there might be more. Reaching the bottom, he once again filled his shirt full of the moss and made his way back. High above him he could see the Black looking out over the cliffs, his mane whipping in the wind. When he reached the top the stallion was still there. He followed a short distance behind as Alec went back to the spring.

Days passed and gradually the friendship between the boy and the Black grew. The stallion now came at his call and let Alec stroke him while he grazed. One night Alec sat within the warm glow of the fire and watched the stallion munching on the carragheen beside the pool. He wondered if the stallion was as tired of the carragheen as he. Alec had found that if he boiled it in the turtle shell it formed a gelatinous substance which tasted a little better than the raw moss. A fish was now a rare delicacy to him.

The flame's shadows reached out and cast eerie ghostlike patterns on the Black's body. Alec's face became grim as thoughts rushed through his brain. Should he try it tomorrow? Did he dare attempt to ride the Black? Should he wait a few more days? Go ahead—tomorrow. *Don't do it!* Go ahead——

The fire burned low, then smoldered. Yet Alec sat beside the fire, his eyes fixed on that blacker-than-night figure beside the spring.

The next morning he woke from a fitful slumber to find the sun high above. Hurriedly he ate some of the carragheen. Then he looked for the Black, but he was not in sight. Alec whistled, but no answer came. He walked toward the hill. The sun blazed down and the sweat ran from his body. If it would only rain! The last week had been like an oven on the island.

When he reached the top of the hill, he saw the Black at one end of the beach. Again he whistled, and this time there was an answering whistle as the stallion turned his head. Alec walked up the beach toward him.

The Black stood still as he approached. He went cautiously up to him and placed a hand on his neck.

"Steady," he murmured, as the warm skin quivered slightly beneath his hand. The stallion showed neither fear nor hate of him; his large eyes were still turned toward the sea.

For a moment Alec stood with his hand on the Black's neck. Then he walked toward a sand dune a short distance away. The stallion followed. He stepped up the side of the dune, his left hand in the horse's thick mane. The Black's ears pricked forward, his eyes followed the boy nervously—some of the savageness returned to them, his muscles twitched. For a moment Alec was undecided what to do. Then his hands gripped the mane tighter and he threw himself on the Black's back. For a second the stallion stood motionless, then he snorted and plunged; the sand went flying as he doubled in the air. Alec felt the mighty muscles heave, then he was flung through the air, landing heavily on his back. Everything went dark.

Alec regained consciousness to find something warm against his cheek. Slowly he opened his eyes. The stallion was pushing him with his head. Alec tried moving his arms and legs, and found them bruised but not broken. Wearily he got to his feet. The wildness and savageness had once more disappeared in the Black; he looked as though nothing had happened.

Alec waited for a few minutes—then once again led the stallion to the sand dune. His hand grasped the horse's mane. But this time he laid only the upper part of his body on the stallion's back, while he talked soothingly into his ear. The Black flirted his ears back and forth, as he glanced backward with his dark eyes.

"See, I'm not going to hurt you," Alex murmured, knowing it was he who might be hurt. After a few minutes, Alec cautiously slid onto his back. Once again, the stallion snorted and sent the boy flying through the air.

Alec picked himself up from the ground—slower this time. But when he had rested, he whistled for the Black again. The stallion moved toward him. Alec determinedly stepped on the sand dune and once again let the Black feel his weight. Gently he spoke into a large ear, "It's me. I'm not much to carry." He slid onto the stallion's back. One arm slipped around the Black's neck as he half-reared.

Then like a shot from a gun, the Black broke down the beach. His action shifted, and his huge strides seemed to make him fly through the air.

Alec clung to the stallion's mane for his life. The wind screamed by and he couldn't see! Suddenly the Black swerved and headed up the sand dune; he reached the top and then down. The spring was a blur as they whipped by. To the rocks he raced, and then the stallion made a wide circle—his speed never diminishing. Down through a long ravine he rushed. Alec's blurred vision made out a black object in front of them, and in a flash he remembered the deep gully that was there. He felt the stallion gather himself; instinctively he leaned forward and held the Black firm and steady with his hands and knees. Then they were in the air, sailing over the black hole. Alec almost lost his balance when they landed but recovered himself in time to keep from falling off! Once again the stallion reached the beach, his hoofbeats regular and rhythmic on the white sand.

The jump had helped greatly in clearing Alec's mind. He leaned closer to the stallion's ear and kept repeating, "Easy, Black. Easy." The stallion seemed to glide over the sand and then his speed began to lessen. Alec kept talking to him. Slower and slower ran the Black. Gradually he came to a stop. The boy released his grip from the stallion's mane and his arms encircled the Black's neck. He was weak with exhaustion—in no condition for such a ride! Wearily he slipped to the ground. Never had he dreamed a horse could run so fast! The stallion looked at him, his head held high, his large body only slightly covered with sweat.

That night Alec lay wide awake, his body aching with pain, but his heart pounding with excitement. He had ridden the Black! He had conquered this wild, unbroken stallion with kindness. He felt sure that from that day on the Black was his—his alone! But for what—would they ever be rescued? Would he ever see his home again? Alec shook his head. He had promised himself he wouldn't think of that any more.

The next day he mounted the Black again. The horse half-reared but didn't fight him. Alec spoke softly in his ear, and the Black stood still. The Alec touched him lightly on the side, and he walked—a long, loping stride. Far up the beach they went, then Alec tried to turn him by shifting his weight, and gently pushing the stallion's head. Gradually the horse turned. Alec took a firmer grip on his long mane and pressed his knees tighter against the large body. The stallion broke out of his walk into a fast canter. The wind blew his mane back into the boy's face. The stallion's stride was effortless, and Alec found it easy to ride. Halfway down the beach, he managed to bring him back again to a walk, then to a complete stop. Slowly he turned him to the right, then to the left, and then around in a circle.

Long but exciting hours passed as Alec tried to make the Black understand what he wanted him to do. The sun was going down rapidly when he walked the stallion to the end of the beach. The Black turned and stood still; a mile of smooth, white sand stretched before them.

Suddenly the stallion bolted, almost throwing Alec to the ground. He picked up speed with amazing swiftness. Faster and faster he went. Alec hung low over his neck, his breath coming in gasps. Down the beach the stallion thundered. Tears from the wind rolled down Alec's cheeks. Three-quarters of the way, he tried to check the Black's speed. He pulled back on the flowing mane. "Whoa, Black," he yelled, but his words were whipped away in the wind.

Swiftly the stallion neared the end of the beach, and Alec thought that his breathtaking ride of yesterday was to be repeated. He pulled back harder on the mane. Suddenly the Black's pace lessened. Alec flung one arm around the stallion's neck. The Black shifted into his fast trot, which gradually became slower and slower, until Alec had him under control. Overjoyed he turned him, and rode him over the hill to the spring. Together they drank the cool, refreshing water.

With the days that followed, Alec's mastery over the Black grew greater and greater. He could do almost anything with him. The savage fury of the unbroken stallion disappeared when he saw the boy. Alec rode him around the island and raced him down the beach,

marveling at the giant strides and the terrific speed. Without realizing it, Alec was improving his horsemanship until he had reached the point where he was almost a part of the Black as they tore along.

One night Alec sat beside his campfire and stared into the flames that reached hungrily into the air; his knees were crossed and his elbows rested heavily upon them, his chin was cupped in his two hands. He was deep in thought. The *Drake* had left Bombay on a Saturday, the fifteenth of August. The shipwreck had happened a little over two weeks later, perhaps on the second of September. He had been on the island exactly—nineteen days. That would make it approximately the twenty-first of September. By now his family must think him dead! He doubled his fists. He had to find a way out; a ship just had to pass the island sometime. Daily he had stood on top of the hill peering out to sea, frantically hoping to sight a boat.

For the first time, Alec thought of the approaching cold weather. The heat had been so intense upon the island since his arrival that it had never entered his mind that it would soon get cold. Would his shelter offer him enough protection? He had used every available piece of wood on the island to reinforce it, but would that be enough? How cold would it get? Alec looked up at the clear, starlit sky.

He rose to his feet and walked toward the hill. The Black, standing beside the spring, raised his head and whistled when he saw him. He followed Alec as he climbed to the top. The boy's eyes swept the dark, rolling sea. White-crested swells rushed in and rolled up the beach. The stallion, too, seemed to be watching—his eyes staring into the night, his ears pricking forward. An hour passed, then they turned and made their way back to camp.

A wind started blowing from out of the west. Alec stoked the fire for the night, then crawled wearily into his shelter. He was tired, for he had spent most of the day gathering carragheen. He stretched out and was soon asleep.

He didn't know how long he had been sleeping, but suddenly the Black's shrill scream awakened him. Sleepily he opened his eyes; the air had grown hot. Then he heard a crackling noise above; his head jerked upward. The top of the shelter was on fire! Flames were creeping down the sides. Alec leaped to his feet and rushed outside.

A gale was sweeping the island and instantly he realized what had happened. Sparks from his campfire had been blown upon the top of the shelter and had easily set fire to the dry wood. He grabbed the turtle shell and ran to the spring. Filling it, he ran back and threw the water on the flames.

The Black pranced nervously beside the spring, his nostrils quivering, while Alec rushed back and forth with his little turtle shell full of water, tying to keep the fire from spreading. But it had a good start and soon it had enveloped the whole shelter. Smoke filled the air. The boy and the horse were forced to move farther and farther back.

Soon the two nearby trees caught. Alec knew that the fire could not spread much farther—the island was too barren of any real fuel. But right now the flames were devouring everything in sight. They roared and reached high into the air. There was nothing that Alec could do. The one thing he really needed—his shelter—was gone. And there was no more wood.

The fire burned a long time before it started to die down. Then the wind too began to diminish. Alec sat beside the spring, watching the flames, until the first streaks of dawn appeared in the sky. He blinked his smoke-filled eyes, gritted his teeth—he wasn't licked yet! He'd find some way to make a shelter, and if that wasn't possible, then he'd sleep outside like the Black.

Determinedly he set out for the beach. Perhaps some wood had been swept ashore during the night. The Black trotted ahead of him. Then Alec saw him snort and rear as he reached the top of the hill, and plunge back down again. Alec hurried forward. From the crest of the hill, he looked down. Below him was a ship anchored four hundred yards off the island!

He heard voices. He saw a rowboat being drawn up on the beach by five men. Incredulous, unable to shout, he rushed down the hill.

"You were right, Pat, there *is* someone on this island!" he heard one of the men shout to the other.

And the other replied in a thick Irish brogue, "Sure, and I knew I saw a fire reaching into the heavens!"

THE CIRCUIT

Francisco Jiménez

It was that time of year again. Ito, the strawberry
sharecropper, did not smile. It was natural. The peak of
the strawberry season was over and the last few days the
workers, most of them *braceros*, were not picking as many
boxes as they had during the months of June and July.

As the last days of August disappeared, so did the
number of braceros. Sunday, only one—the best picker—
came to work. I liked him. Sometimes we talked during
our half-hour lunch break. That is how I found out he was
from Jalisco, the same state in Mexico my family was from.
That Sunday was the last time I saw him.

When the sun had tired and sunk behind the
mountains, Ito signaled us that it was time to go home.
"Ya esora," he yelled in his broken Spanish. Those were
the words I waited for twelve hours a day, everyday,
seven days a week, week after week. And the thought of
not hearing them again saddened me.

As we drove home Papa did not say a word. With
both hands on the wheel, he stared at the dirt road. My
older brother, Roberto, was also silent. He leaned his head
back and closed his eyes. Once in a while he cleared from
his throat the dust that blew in from outside.

Yes, it was that time of year. When I opened the front
door to the shack, I stopped. Everything we owned was
neatly packed in cardboard boxes. Suddenly I felt even
more the weight of hours, days, weeks, and months of
work. I sat down on a box. The thought of having to move
to Fresno and knowing what was in store for me there
brought tears to my eyes.

That night I could not sleep. I lay in bed thinking about how much I hated this move.

A little before five o'clock in the morning, Papa woke everyone up. A few minutes later, the yelling and screaming of my little brothers and sisters, for whom the move was a great adventure, broke the silence of dawn. Shortly, the barking of the dogs accompanied them.

While we packed the breakfast dishes, Papa went outside to start the "Carcanchita." That was the name Papa gave his old '38 black Plymouth. He bought it in a used-car lot in Santa Rosa in the winter of 1949. Papa was very proud of his car. "Mi Carcanchita," my little jalopy, he called it. He had a right to be proud of it. He spent a lot of time looking at other cars before buying this one. When he finally chose the "Carcanchita," he checked it thoroughly before driving it out of the car lot. He examined every inch of the car. He listened to the motor, tilting his head from side to side like a parrot, trying to detect any noises that spelled car trouble. After being satisfied with the looks and sounds of the car, Papa then insisted on knowing who the original owner was. He never did find out from the car salesman. But he bought the car anyway. Papa figured the original owner must have been an important man because behind the rear seat of the car he found a blue necktie.

Papa parked the car out in front and left the motor running. *"Listo"* (ready), he yelled. Without saying a word, Roberto and I began to carry the boxes out to the car. Roberto carried the two big boxes and I carried the two smaller ones. Papa then threw the mattress on top of the car roof and tied it with ropes to the front and rear bumpers.

Everything was packed except Mama's pot. It was an old large galvanized pot she had picked up at an army surplus store in Santa Maria the year I was born. The pot was full of dents and nicks, and the more dents and nicks it had, the more Mama liked it. *"Mi olla"* (my pot), she used to say proudly.

I held the front door open as Mama carefully carried out her pot by both handles, making sure not to spill the cooked beans. When she got to the car, Papa reached out to help her with it. Roberto opened the rear car door and Papa gently placed it on the floor behind the front seat. All of us then climbed in. Papa sighed, wiped the sweat off his forehead with his sleeve, and said wearily: *"Es todo"* (that's it).

As we drove away, I felt a lump in my throat. I turned around and looked at our little shack for the last time.

At sunset we drove into a labor camp near Fresno. Since Papa did not speak English, Mama asked the camp foreman if he needed any more workers. "We don't need no more," said the foreman, scratching his head. "Check with Sullivan down the road. Can't miss him. He lives in a big white house with a fence around it."

When we got there, Mama walked up to the house. She went through a white gate, past a row of rose bushes, up the stairs to the front door. She rang the doorbell. The porch light went on and a tall husky man came out. They exchanged a few words. After the man went in, Mama clasped her hands and hurried back to the car. "We have work! Mr. Sullivan said we can stay there the whole season," she said gasping and pointing to an old garage near the stables.

The garage was worn out by the years. It had no windows. The walls, eaten by termites, strained to support the roof full of holes. The loose dirt floor, populated by earthworms, looked like a gray road map.

That night, by the light of a kerosene lamp, we unpacked and cleaned our new home. Roberto swept away the loose dirt, leaving the hard ground. Papa plugged the holes in the walls with old newspapers and tin can tops. Mama fed my little brothers and sisters. Papa and Roberto then brought in the mattress and placed it on the far corner of the garage. "Mama, you and the little ones sleep on the mattress. Roberto, Panchito, and I will sleep outside under the trees," Papa said.

Early next morning Mr. Sullivan showed us where his crop was, and after breakfast, Papa, Roberto, and I headed for the vineyard to pick.

Around nine o'clock the temperature had risen to almost one hundred degrees. I was completely soaked in sweat and my mouth felt as if I had been chewing on a handkerchief. I walked over to the end of the row, picked up the jug of water we had brought, and began drinking. "Don't drink too much; you'll get sick," Roberto shouted. No sooner had he said that than I felt sick to my stomach. I dropped to my knees and let the jug roll off my hands. I remained motionless with my eyes glued on the hot sandy ground. All I could hear was the drone of insects. Slowly I began to recover. I poured water over my face and neck and watched the black mud run down my arms and hit the ground.

I still felt a little dizzy when we took a break to eat lunch. It was past two o'clock and we sat underneath a large walnut tree that was on the side of the road. While we ate, Papa jotted down the number of boxes we had picked. Roberto drew designs on the ground with a stick. Suddenly I noticed Papa's face turn pale as he looked down the road. "Here comes the school bus," he whispered loudly in alarm. Instinctively, Roberto and I ran and hid in the vineyards. We did not want to get in trouble for not going to school. The yellow bus stopped in front of Mr. Sullivan's house. Two neatly dressed boys about my age got off. They carried books under their arms. After they crossed the street, the bus drove away. Roberto and I came out from hiding and joined Papa. *"Tienen que tener cuidado"* (you have to be careful), he warned us.

After lunch we went back to work. The sun kept beating down. The buzzing insects, the wet sweat, and the hot dry dust made the afternoon seem to last forever. Finally the mountains around the valley reached out and swallowed the sun. Within an hour it was too dark to continue picking. The vines blanketed the grapes, making it difficult to see the bunches. *"Vámonos,"* said Papa, signaling to us that it was time to quit work. Papa then took out a pencil and began to figure out how much we had earned our first day. He wrote down numbers, crossed some out, wrote down some more. *"Quince"* (fifteen dollars), he murmured.

When we arrived home, we took a cold shower underneath a waterhose. We then sat down to eat dinner around some wooden crates that served as a table. Mama had cooked a special meal for us. We had rice and tortillas with *carne con chile*, my favorite dish.

The next morning I could hardly move. My body ached all over. I felt little control over my arms and legs. This feeling went on every morning for days until my muscles finally got used to the work.

It was Monday, the first week of November. The grape season was over and I could now go to school. I woke up early that morning and lay in bed, looking at the stars and savoring the thought of not going to work and of starting sixth grade for the first time that year. Since I could not sleep, I decided to get up and join Papa and Roberto at breakfast. I sat at the table across from Roberto, but I kept my head down. I did not want to look up and face him. I knew he was sad. He was not going to school today. He was not going tomorrow, or next week, or next month. He would not go until the cotton season was over, and that was sometime in February. I rubbed my hands together and watched the dry, acid-stained skin fall to the floor in little rolls.

When Papa and Roberto left for work, I felt relief. I walked to the top of a small grade next to the shack and watched the "Carcanchita" disappear in the distance in a cloud of dust.

Two hours later, around eight o'clock, I stood by the side of the road waiting for school bus number twenty. When it arrived I climbed in. No one noticed me. Everyone was busy either talking or yelling. I sat in an empty seat in the back.

When the bus stopped in front of the school, I felt very nervous. I looked out the bus window and saw boys and girls carrying books under their arms. I felt empty. I put my hands in my pants pockets and walked to the principal's office. When I entered I heard a woman's voice say: "May I help you?" I was startled. I had not heard English for months. For a few seconds I remained speechless. I looked at the lady who waited for an answer.

My first instinct was to answer her in Spanish, but I held back. Finally, after struggling for English words I managed to tell her that I wanted to enroll in the sixth grade. After answering many questions, I was led to the classroom.

Mr. Lema, the sixth-grade teacher, greeted me and assigned me a desk. He then introduced me to the class. I was so nervous and scared at that moment when everyone's eyes were on me that I wished I were with Papa and Roberto picking cotton. After taking roll, Mr. Lema gave the class the assignment for the first hour. "The first thing we have to do this morning is finish reading the story we began yesterday," he said enthusiastically. He walked up to me, handed me an English book, and asked me to read. "We are on page 125," he said politely. When I heard this, I felt my blood rush to my head; I felt dizzy. "Would you like to read?" he asked hesitantly. I opened the book to page 125. My mouth was dry. My eyes began to water. I could not begin. "You can read later," Mr. Lema said understandingly.

For the rest of the reading period I kept getting angrier and angrier with myself. I should have read, I thought to myself.

During recess I went into the restroom and opened my English book to page 125. I began to read in a low voice, pretending I was in class. There were many words I did not know. I closed the book and headed back to the classroom.

Mr. Lema was sitting at his desk correcting papers. When I entered he looked up at me and smiled. I felt better. I walked up to him and asked if he could help me with the new words. "Gladly," he said.

The rest of the month I spent my lunch hours working on English with Mr. Lema, my best friend at school.

One Friday during lunch hour Mr. Lema asked me to take a walk with him to the music room. "Do you like music?" he asked me as we entered the building.

"Yes, I like Mexican *corridos*," I answered. He then picked up a trumpet, blew on it and handed it to me. The sound gave me goose bumps. I knew that sound. I had heard it in many Mexican corridos. "How would you like to learn how to play it?" he asked. He must have read my face because before I could answer, he added: "I'll teach you how to play it during our lunch hours."

That day I could hardly wait to get home to tell Papa and Mama the great news. As I got off the bus, my little brothers and sisters ran up to meet me. They were yelling and screaming. I thought they were happy to see me, but when I opened the door to our shack, I saw that everything we owned was neatly packed in cardboard boxes.

PRIMER LESSON

Carl Sandburg

Look out how you use proud words.
When you let proud words go,
   it is not easy to call them back.
They wear long boots, hard boots;
   they walk off proud; they can't hear you
   calling—
Look out how you use proud words.

Vision of a Past Warrior

Peter La Farge

I have within me such a dream of pain
That all my silver horseman hopes rust still,
Beyond quicksilver mountains,
On the plain,
The buffalo are gone,
None left to kill,

I see the plains grow blackened with that dawn,
No robes for winter warmth
No meat to eat,
The ghost white buffalo's medicine gone,
No hope for Indians then,
I see defeat.

Then there will be changes to another way,
We will fight battles that are legends long.
But of all our glory
None will stay,
Who will remember
That I sang this song.

Thank You, M'am

Langston Hughes

She was a large woman with a large purse that had everything in it but a hammer and nails. It had a long strap, and she carried it slung across her shoulder. It was about eleven o'clock at night, dark, and she was walking alone, when a boy ran up behind her and tried to snatch her purse. The strap broke with the sudden single tug the boy gave it from behind. But the boy's weight and the weight of the purse combined caused him to lose his balance. Instead of taking off full blast as he had hoped, the boy fell on his back on the sidewalk, and his legs flew up. The large woman simply turned around and kicked him right square in his blue-jeaned sitter. Then she reached down, picked the boy up by his shirt front, and shook him until his teeth rattled.

After that the woman said, "Pick up my pocketbook, boy, and give it here."

She still held him tightly. But she bent down enough

to permit him to stoop and pick up her purse. Then she said, "Now ain't you ashamed of yourself?"

Firmly gripped by his shirt front, the boy said, "Yes'm."

The woman said, "What did you want to do it for?"

The boy said, "I didn't aim to."

She said, "You a lie!"

By that time two or three people passed, stopped, turned to look, and some stood watching.

"If I turn you loose, will you run?" asked the woman.

"Yes'm," said the boy.

"Then I won't turn you loose," said the woman. She did not release him.

"Lady, I'm sorry," whispered the boy.

"Um-hum! Your face is dirty. I got a great mind to wash your face for you. Ain't you got nobody home to tell you to wash your face?"

"No'm," said the boy.

"Then it will get washed this evening," said the large woman, starting up the street, dragging the frightened boy behind her.

He looked as if he were fourteen or fifteen, frail and willow-wild, in tennis shoes and blue jeans.

The woman said, "You ought to be my son. I would teach you right from wrong. Least I can do right now is to wash your face. Are you hungry?"

"No'm," said the being-dragged boy. "I just want you to turn me loose."

"Was I bothering *you* when I turned that corner?" asked the woman.

"No'm."

"But you put yourself in contact with *me*," said the woman. "If you think that that contact is not going to last a while, you got another thought coming. When I get through with you, sir, you are going to remember Mrs. Luella Bates Washington Jones."

Sweat popped out on the boy's face, and he began to struggle. Mrs. Jones stopped, jerked him around in front of her, put a half nelson around his neck, and continued to drag him up the street. When she got to her door, she dragged the boy inside, down a hall, and into a large kitchenette-furnished room at the rear of the house. She switched on the light and left the door open. The boy could hear other roomers laughing and talking in the large house. Some of their doors were open, too, so he knew he and the woman were not alone. The woman still had him by the neck in the middle of her room.

She said, "What is your name?"

"Roger," answered the boy.

"Then, Roger, you go to that sink and wash your face," said the woman, whereupon she turned him loose—at last. Roger looked at the door—looked at the woman—looked at the door—*and went to the sink.*

"Let the water run until it gets warm," she said. "Here's a clean towel."

"You gonna take me to jail?" asked the boy, bending over the sink.

"Not with that face, I would not take you nowhere," said the woman. "Here I am trying to get home to cook me a bite to eat, and you snatch my pocketbook! Maybe you ain't been to your supper either, late as it be. Have you?"

"There's nobody home at my house," said the boy.

"Then we'll eat," said the woman. "I believe you're hungry—or been hungry—to try to snatch my pocketbook!"

"I want a pair of blue suede shoes," said the boy.

"Well, you didn't have to snatch *my* pocketbook to get some suede shoes," said Mrs. Luella Bates Washington Jones. "You could of asked me."

"M'am?"

The water dripping from his face, the boy looked at her. There was a long pause. A very long pause. After he had dried his face, and not knowing what else to do, dried it again, the boy turned around, wondering what next. The door was open. He could make a dash for it down the hall. He could run, run, run, *run!*

The woman was sitting on the daybed. After a while she said, "I were young once, and I wanted things I could not get."

There was another long pause. The boy's mouth opened. Then he frowned, not knowing he frowned.

The woman said, "Um-hum! You thought I was going to say *but,* didn't you? You thought I was going to say *but I didn't snatch people's pocketbooks.* Well, I wasn't going to say that." Pause. Silence. "I have done things, too, which I would not tell you, son—neither tell God, if He didn't already know. Everybody's got something in common. So you set down while I fix us something to eat. You might run that comb through your hair so you will look presentable."

In another corner of the room behind a screen was a gas plate and an icebox. Mrs. Jones got up and went behind the screen. The woman did not watch the boy to see if he was going to run now, nor did she watch her purse, which she left behind her on the daybed. But the boy took care to sit on the far side of the room, away from the purse, where he thought she could easily see him out of the corner of her eye if she wanted to. He did not trust the woman *not* to trust him. And he did not want to be mistrusted now.

"Do you need somebody to go to the store," asked the boy, "maybe to get some milk or something?"

"Don't believe I do," said the woman, "unless you just want sweet milk yourself. I was going to make cocoa out of this canned milk I got here."

"That will be fine," said the boy.

She heated some lima beans and ham she had in the icebox, made the cocoa, and set the table. The woman did not ask the boy anything about where he lived, or his folks, or anything else that would embarrass him. Instead, as they ate, she told him about her job in a hotel beauty shop that stayed open late, what the work was like, and how all kinds of women came in and out, blondes, redheads, and Spanish. Then she cut him a half of her ten-cent cake.

"Eat some more, son," she said.

When they were finished eating, she got up and said, "Now here, take this ten dollars and buy yourself some blue suede shoes. And next time, do not make the mistake of latching onto *my* pocketbook *nor nobody else's*—because shoes got by devilish ways will burn your feet. I got to get my rest now. But from here on in, son, I hope you will behave yourself."

She led him down the hall to the front door and opened it. "Good night! Behave yourself, boy!" she said, looking out into the street as he went down the steps.

The boy wanted to say something other than, "Thank you, m'am," to Mrs. Luella Bates Washington Jones, but although his lips moved, he couldn't even say that as he turned at the foot of the barren stoop and looked up at the large woman in the door. Then she shut the door.

THE
BIG
WAVE

•

Pearl S. Buck

There was much in life to enjoy. Kino had a good time every day. In the winter he went to a school in the fishing village, and he and Jiya shared a seat. They studied reading and arithmetic and all the things that other children learn in school. But in the summer Kino had to work hard on the farm, for his father needed help. Even Setsu and the mother helped when the rice seedlings had to be planted

in the flooded fields on the terraces, and they helped, too, when the grain was ripe and had to be cut into sheaves and threshed. On those days Kino could not run down the mountainside to find Jiya. When the day was over he was so tired he fell asleep over his supper.

But there were days when Jiya also was too busy to play. Word came in from the fishermen up the coast that a school of fish was passing through the channels and then every fishing boat made haste to sail out of the bays and inlets into the main currents of the sea. Early in the morning, sometimes so early that the light was still that of the setting moon, Jiya and his father sailed their boat out across the silvery sea, to let down their nets at dawn. If they were lucky the nets came up so heavy with fish that it took all their strength to haul them up, and soon the bottom of the boat was flashing and sparkling with the wriggling fish.

Sometimes, if it was not seedtime or harvest, Kino went with Jiya and his father. It was an exciting thing to get up in the night and dress himself in his warm padded jacket tied around his waist. Even in summer the wind was cool over the sea at dawn. However early he got up, his mother always got up too, and gave him a bowl of hot rice soup and some bean curd and hot tea before he started. Then she packed his lunch in a clean little wooden box, cold rice and fish and a bit of radish pickle.

Down the stone steps of the mountain path Kino ran straight to the narrow dock where the fishing boats bobbed up and down on the tide. Jiya and his father were already there, and in a few minutes the boat was nosing its way between the rocks out to the open sea. Sails set and filling with the wind, they sped straight into the dawn-lit sky. Kino crouched down on the floor behind the bow and felt his heart rise with joy and excitement. The shore fell far behind them and the boat took on the deep swell of the ocean. Soon they came to a whole fleet of fishing boats, and then together they flew after the schools of fish. It was like being a bird in a flock, flying into the sky. How exciting it was, too, to pull up the fish! At such times Kino felt Jiya was more lucky than he. Fish harvest was much easier than rice harvest.

"I wish my father were a fisherman," he would tell Jiya. "It is stupid to plow and plant and cut the sheaves, when I could just come out like this and reap fish from the sea."

Jiya shook his head. "But when the storms come, you wish yourself back upon the earth," he said. Then he laughed. "How would fish taste without rice? Think of eating only fish!"

"We need both farmers and fishermen," Jiya's father said.

On days when the sky was bright and the winds mild the ocean lay so calm and blue that it was hard to believe that it could be cruel and angry. Yet even Kino never quite forgot that under the warm blue surface the water was cold and green. When the sun shone the deep water was still. But when the deep water moved and heaved and stirred, ah, then Kino was glad that his father was a farmer and not a fisherman.

And yet, one day, it was the earth that brought the big wave. Deep under the deepest part of the ocean, miles under the still green waters, fires raged in the heart of the earth. The icy cold of the water could not chill those fires. Rocks were melted and boiled under the crust of the ocean's bed, under the weight of the water, but they could not break through. At last the steam grew so strong that it forced its way through to the mouth of the volcano. That day, as he helped his father plant turnips, Kino saw the sky overcast halfway to the zenith.

"Look, Father!" he cried. "The volcano is burning again!"

His father stopped and gazed anxiously at the sky. "It looks very angry," he said. "I shall not sleep tonight."

All night while the others slept, Kino's father kept watch. When it was dark, the sky was lit with red and the earth trembled under the farmhouses. Down at the fishing village lights in the little houses showed that other people watched, too. For generations people had watched earth and sea.

Morning came, a strange fiery dawn. The sky was red and gray, and even here upon the farms cinders and ash fell from the volcano. Kino had a strange feeling, when he stepped barefoot upon the earth, that it was hot under his feet. In the house the mother had taken down everything from the walls that could fall or be broken, and her few good dishes she had packed into straw in a basket and set outside.

"Shall we have an earthquake, Father?" Kino asked as they ate breakfast.

"I cannot tell, my son," his father replied. "Earth and sea are struggling together against the fires inside the earth."

No fishing boats set sail that hot summer morning. There was no wind. The sea lay dead and calm, as though oil had been poured upon the waters. It was a purple gray, suave and beautiful, but when Kino looked at it he felt afraid.

"Why is the sea such a color?" he asked.

"Sea mirrors sky," his father replied. "Sea and earth and sky—if they work together against people, it will be dangerous indeed for us."

"Where are the gods at such a time?" Kino asked. "Will they not be mindful of us?"

"There are times when the gods leave people to take care of

themselves," his father replied. "They test us, to see how able we are to save ourselves."

"And if we are not able?" Kino asked.

"We must be able," his father replied. "Fear alone makes a person weak. If you are afraid, your hands tremble, your feet falter, and your brain cannot tell hands and feet what to do."

No one stirred from home that day. Kino's father sat at the door, watching the sky and the oily sea, and Kino stayed near him. He did not know what Jiya was doing, but he imagined that Jiya, too, stayed by his father. So the hours passed until noon.

At noon his father pointed down the mountainside. "Look at Old Gentleman's castle," he said.

Halfway down the mountainside on the knoll where the castle stood, Kino now saw a red flag rise slowly to the top of a tall pole and hang limp against the gray sky.

"Old Gentleman is telling everyone to be ready," Kino's father went on. "Twice have I seen that flag go up, both times before you were born."

"Be ready for what?" Kino asked in a frightened voice.

"For whatever happens," Kino's father replied.

At two o'clock the sky began to grow black. The air was as hot as though a forest fire were burning, but there was no sign of such a fire. The glow of the volcano glared over the mountaintop, blood-red against the black. A deep-toned bell tolled over the hills.

"What is that bell?" Kino asked his father. "I never heard it before."

"It rang twice before you were born," his father replied. "It is the bell in the temple inside the walls of Old Gentleman's castle. He is calling the people to come up out of the village and shelter within his walls."

"Will they come?" Kino asked.

"Not all of them," his father replied. "Parents will try to make their children go, but the children will not want to leave their parents. Mothers will not want to leave fathers, and the fathers will stay by their boats. But some will want to be sure of life."

The bell kept on ringing urgently, and soon out of the village a trickling stream of people, nearly all of them children, began to climb toward the knoll.

"I wish Jiya would come," Kino said. "Do you think he will see me if I stand on the edge of the terrace and wave my white girdle cloth?"

"Try it," his father said.

"Come with me," Kino begged.

So Kino and his father stood on the edge of the terrace and waved. Kino took off the strip of white cloth from about his waist that he wore instead of a belt, and he waved it, holding it in both hands, high above his head.

Far down the hill Jiya saw the two figures and the waving strip of white against the dark sky. He was crying as he climbed, and trying not to cry. He had not wanted to leave his father, but because he was the youngest one, his older brother and his father and mother had all told him that he must go up the mountain. "We must divide ourselves," Jiya's father said. "If the ocean yields to the fires you must live after us."

"I don't want to live alone," Jiya said.

"It is your duty to obey me, as a good Japanese son," his father told him.

Jiya had run out of the house, crying. Now when he saw Kino, he decided that he would go there instead of to the castle, and he began to hurry up the hill to the farm. Next to his own family he loved Kino's strong father and kind mother. He had no sister of his own and he thought Setsu was the prettiest girl he had ever seen.

Kino's father put out his hand to help Jiya up the stone wall and Kino was just about to shout out his welcome when suddenly a hurricane wind broke out of the ocean. Kino and Jiya clung together and wrapped their arms about the father's waist.

"Look—look—what is that?" Kino screamed.

The purple rim of the ocean seemed to lift and rise against the clouds. A silver-green band of bright sky appeared like a low dawn above the sea.

"May the gods save us," Kino heard his father mutter. The castle bell began to toll again, deep and pleading. Ah, but would the people hear it in the roaring wind? Their houses had no windows toward the sea. Did they know what was about to happen?

Under the deep waters of the ocean, miles down under the cold, the earth had yielded at last to the fire. It groaned and split open and the cold water fell into the middle of the boiling rocks. Steam burst out and lifted the ocean high into the sky in a big wave. It rushed toward the shore, green and solid, frothing into white at its edges. It rose, higher and higher, lifting up hands and claws.

"I must tell my father!" Jiya screamed.

But Kino's father held him fast with both arms. "It is too late," he said sternly.

And he would not let Jiya go.

In a few seconds, before their eyes the wave had grown and come nearer and nearer, higher and higher. The air was filled with its roar and shout. It rushed over the flat still waters of the ocean and before Jiya could scream again it reached the village and covered it fathoms deep in swirling wild

water, green laced with fierce white foam. The wave ran up the mountainside, until the knoll where the castle stood was an island. All who were still climbing the path were swept away—black, tossing scraps in the wicked waters. The wave ran up the mountain until Kino and Jiya saw the wavelets curl at the terrace walls upon which they stood. Then with a great sucking sigh, the wave swept back again, ebbing into the ocean, dragging everything with it, trees and stones and houses. They stood, the man and the two boys, utterly silent, clinging together, facing the wave as it went away. It swept back over the village and returned slowly again to the ocean, subsiding, sinking into a great stillness.

Upon the beach where the village stood not a house remained, no wreckage of wood or fallen stone wall, no little street of shops, no docks, not a single boat. The beach was as clean of houses as if no human beings had ever lived there. All that had been was now no more.

Jiya gave a wild cry and Kino felt him slip to the ground. He was unconscious. What he had seen was too much for him. What he knew, he could not bear. His family and his home were gone.

Kino began to cry and Kino's father did not stop him. He stooped and gathered Jiya into his arms and carried him into the house, and

Kino's mother ran out of the kitchen and put down a mattress and Kino's father laid Jiya upon it.

"It is better that he is unconscious," he said gently. "Let him remain so until his own will wakes him. I will sit by him."

"I will rub his hands and feet," Kino's mother said sadly.

Kino could say nothing. He was still crying and his father let him cry for a while. Then he said to his wife, "Heat a little rice soup for Kino and put ginger in it. He feels cold."

Now Kino did not know until his father spoke that he did feel cold. He was shivering and he could not stop crying. Setsu came in. She had not seen the big wave, for her mother had closed the windows and drawn the curtains against the sea. But now she saw Jiya lying white-pale and still.

"Is Jiya dead?" she asked.

"No, Jiya is living," her father replied.

"Why doesn't he open his eyes?" she asked again.

"Soon he will open his eyes," the father replied.

"If Jiya is not dead, why does Kino cry?" Setsu asked.

"You are asking too many questions," her father told her.

So Setsu left the room, sucking her forefinger, and staring at Jiya and Kino as she went, and soon the mother came in with the hot rice soup and Kino drank it. He felt warm now and he could stop crying. But he was still frightened and sad.

"What will we say to Jiya when he wakes?" he asked his father.

"We will not talk," his father replied. "We will give him warm food and let him rest. We will help him to feel he still has a home."

"Here?" Kino asked.

"Yes," his father replied. "I have always wanted another son, and Jiya will be that son. As soon as he knows that this is his home, then we must help him to understand what has happened."

excerpt from

The Wright Brothers

Quentin Reynolds

Kitty Hawk

Wilbur and Orville Wright built the first successful airplane and flew it for the first time in December 1903. They prepared for this first triumphant flight by studying the principles of flight and building several gliders—flying machines without engines that depended on the wind to move them into and through the air. This account tells of the Wright brothers' first glider flight at Kitty Hawk, North Carolina in 1900.

Today you could get on an airplane at Dayton and be at Kitty Hawk in less than two hours. But it took Wilbur and Orv a week to reach the lonely fishing hamlet. Kitty Hawk is about sixty miles from Cape Hatteras, which is one of the stormiest places on the Atlantic Coast. But it is rarely stormy at Kitty Hawk. It is a place of sand dunes and gentle hills and no trees at all.

"This is perfect," Wilbur said. "And best of all, there are scarcely any people here. Nobody will think we're crazy when we start flying our glider."

They had brought a tent with them and they put it up. Kate had packed a suitcase with jelly and jam and other foods she always canned at home. Will and Orv had brought all of their precious books and pamphlets and all kinds of tools with them, and now they were ready for the big test.

Kitty Hawk, the scene of their test, consisted of
nothing but a government weather bureau and a life-saving
station, but because of these it had a post office. This was
run by Mr. William Tate, and Will and Orv arranged with
Mrs. Tate to have their meals with the family.

As they assembled their glider, there was no one to
laugh at them but a few seagulls hovering above. The

glider was just a big box kite with an upper and a lower wing. Mr. Tate (who only had four or five letters a day to deliver) looked at it curiously, but he didn't laugh. There was something about these two serious-eyed young men that kept a person from laughing. Mr. Tate, in fact, asked if he could help them.

Well, they needed a helper. They had reached the point where they had "studied the way to ride a horse," and now they had to climb on its back and see if they could stay on. One of them would ride the glider, but two others were needed to run ahead and give it a start. This glider had to be pulled along just as a kite was pulled along, until the wind grabbed it and took it up into the air. They tossed a coin and Orville won. He'd be the first rider.

Otto Lilienthal and the other glider experts always sat upright on the lower wing of the gliders. Wilbur remembered the first time his mother had used the expression "wind resistance," and he remembered how fast his sled had gone when he had lain on it. And of course he remembered how fast Orville had gone on his bike when he had lowered the handlebars and leaned over to "get under the wind."

"Lie down on the wing, Orv," Will said. "That'll reduce the wind resistance."

Orv nodded and took his place. The glider was nestled on top of a sand dune. Wilbur and Mr. Tate stood on either side of it. Wilbur had attached strong cords to each side of the glider, and he and Mr. Tate grabbed the loose ends.

"We'll pull the glider downhill," Will explained to Mr. Tate. "And then . . . well . . . maybe it'll go up into the air. Ready? One . . . two . . . three . . . GO!"

They trotted down the sand dune, pulling the light glider along. Nothing happened. They ran now faster and faster, and suddenly there was a yell from Orville.

"I'm flying," he cried and, sure enough, the glider was about five feet off the ground. It rose to eight feet, and now Wilbur and Mr. Tate dropped the cords they'd been holding. The glider went beautifully for about a hundred feet—and then a gust of wind took it and almost turned it over. A down draft then sent the glider crashing to the ground. Orv wasn't hurt, but the glider was. But the Wrights didn't care.

"We built a kite that took us into the air!" Orv cried with excitement.

"Now let's fix it and try again," Wilbur said.

Mr. Tate noticed that the cloth was ripped in several places. "Can either of you young men run a sewing machine?" he asked.

"Why sure, Mr. Tate," Orv said.

"Well, Mrs. Tate has a nice new sewing machine she'll be glad to let you borrow," Mr. Tate said. "It'd be a lot quicker than sewing up those . . . those wings . . . by hand."

Wings? Even Mr. Tate was using the word. Orv had flown on wings. Let others call it a big box kite or even a glider. He knew that he had flown on wings. He'd only flown for about ten seconds, but he had flown.

The next day it was Wilbur's turn. He stayed up a little longer. Every day now the Wrights tried out their glider. Whichever one was on the ground took notes of what was happening. They found out a great many things. They discovered that if the wind was right, they could actually go about ten miles an hour. They had always believed that balance was the most important thing in kite flying, or, for that matter, in any kind of flying. And their glider had no balance. Whenever a gust of wind hit it, the glider would either turn halfway over or plummet to the ground.

"When the right side of the glider dips, try to shift over to the left side," Wilbur said thoughtfully. "That might balance it."

On their next flight Orv tried that, but it didn't work very well. Then, too, they could not steer their glider. As Will had once said, a glider was at the mercy of the winds.

Every night after dinner at Mrs. Tate's the Wrights would sit around her kitchen table talking about the mistakes that had been made that day. They wrote them all down. The cloth they had been using was called "sateen" (almost like silk). They felt that it "leaked" air. They'd have to find some cloth that was more airtight.

And somehow or other they'd have to find a way to balance and steer the glider.

"Let's make a rudder like the one we made for our sled years ago," Orv suggested, and Will thought that a good idea.

"We might try a horizontal rudder, though," Orv said. "One that is parallel to the ground. That might make us go up or down. We'll make it so we can adjust it. Tip it one way, we go up. Tip it another, we go down."

Within three days they had built a rudder. But they attached it to the front of the glider, not the back. There was a good reason for that. The person on the glider had to raise or lower the rudder, and if it was in back of him he wouldn't have been able to get at it. Wilbur named it the "front elevating rudder." (Ask a pilot what a front elevating rudder is and he'll point it out to you.)

It was Will's turn to fly now, and again Mr. Tate was on hand to help. The winds were stronger than they had been, for it was November now, and winter was approaching. The glider lifted easily into the air. It rose to fifteen feet and then Wilbur tried the rudder. He pulled the two cords that raised the front of it and immediately the glider zoomed up at least another fifteen feet. Then he pulled the two cords again and the glider nosed down. It nosed down fast. Will tried to yank the cords to raise the rudder, but one of them broke and the glider nose-dived right into a sand dune.

Orv had a sinking feeling as he ran to where the glider and Wilbur lay all mixed up with the sand. But Wilbur wasn't even hurt. He was just stunned a little, and he was smiling.

"We did it!" he cried out. "We made it go up and then down. The wind wasn't the boss."

"But look at the glider," Orv said in dismay. "It's completely wrecked."

"We can build another one, Orv," Will said. "And a better one. Mr. Tate, maybe you can use the cloth."

"Mrs. Tate could use it to make our little girl a dress," Mr. Tate said with a smile.

"We're going to pack up and go home," Will said. "But we'll be back next year."

They did pack up, and the day they left for home the Tates' little daughter came to see them. She was wearing a very pretty dress. She never knew that she was wearing part of the most important glider ever made—the first glider that went up or down at the will of the pilot. It was the first glider that had conquered the air.

Wilbur Wright and Orville Wright

Rosemary and Stephen Vincent Benét

Said Orville Wright to Wilbur Wright,
"These birds are very trying.
I'm sick of hearing them cheep-cheep
About the fun of flying.
A bird has feathers, it is true.
That much I freely grant.
But, must that stop us, W?"
Said Wilbur Wright, "It shan't."

And so they built a glider, first,
And then they built another.
—There never were two brothers more
Devoted to each other.
They ran a dusty little shop
For bicycle-repairing,
And bought each other soda-pop
And praised each other's daring.

They glided here, they glided there,
They sometimes skinned their noses.
—For learning how to rule the air
Was not a bed of roses—
But each would murmur, afterward,
While patching up his bro,
"Are we discouraged, W?"
"Of course we are not, O!"

And finally, at Kitty Hawk
In Nineteen-Three (let's cheer it!),
The first real airplane really flew
With Orville there to steer it!
—And kingdoms may forget their kings
And dogs forget their bites,
But, not till Man forgets his wings,
Will men forget the Wrights.

Imagination is the eye of the soul.

Alice

Shel Silverstein

She drank from a bottle called DRINK ME
And up she grew so tall,
She ate from a plate called TASTE ME
And down she shrank so small.
And so she changed, while other folks
Never tried nothin' at all.

excerpt from *Alice's Adventures in Wonderland*

Lewis Carroll

DOWN THE RABBIT-HOLE

Alice's Adventures in Wonderland is one of the world's most famous books for children. You may have seen the movie based on this book or heard people use expressions such as "grinning like the Cheshire cat" or "as mad as a hatter." The book tells the story of a little girl who falls down a rabbit hole to a land of wonder and fantasy.

Alice was beginning to get very tired of sitting by her sister on the bank, and of having nothing to do: once or twice she had peeped into the book her sister was reading, but it had no pictures or conversations in it, "and what is the use of a book," thought Alice, "without pictures or conversations?"

So she was considering, in her own mind (as well as she could, for the hot day made her feel very sleepy and stupid), whether the pleasure of making a daisy-chain would be worth the trouble of getting up and picking the daisies, when suddenly a White Rabbit with pink eyes ran close by her.

There was nothing so *very* remarkable in that; nor did Alice think it so *very* much out of the way to hear the Rabbit say to itself "Oh dear! Oh dear! I shall be too late!" (when she thought it over afterwards, it occurred to her that she ought to have wondered at this, but at the time it all seemed quite natural); but, when the Rabbit actually *took a watch out of its waistcoat-pocket*, and looked at it, and then hurried on, Alice started to her feet, for it flashed across her mind that she had never before seen a rabbit with either a waistcoat-pocket, or a watch to take out of it, and, burning with curiosity, she ran across the field after it, and was just in time to see it pop down a large rabbit-hole under the hedge.

In another moment down went Alice after it, never once considering how in the world she was to get out again.

The rabbit-hole went straight on like a tunnel for some way, and then dipped suddenly down, so suddenly that Alice had not a moment to think about stopping herself before she found herself falling down what seemed to be a very deep well.

Either the well was very deep, or she fell very slowly, for she had plenty of time as she went down to look about her, and to wonder what was going to happen next. First, she tried to look down and make out what she was coming to, but it was too dark to see anything: then she looked at the sides of the well, and noticed that they were filled with cupboards and book-shelves: here and there she saw maps and pictures hung upon pegs. She took down a jar from one of the shelves as she passed: it was labeled "ORANGE MARMALADE," but to her great disappointment it was empty: she did not like to drop the jar, for fear of killing somebody underneath, so managed to put it into one of the cupboards as she fell past it.

"Well!" thought Alice to herself. "After such a fall as this, I shall think nothing of tumbling down-stairs! How brave they'll all think me at home! Why, I wouldn't say anything about it, even if I fell off the top of the house!" (Which was very likely true.)

Down, down, down. Would the fall *never* come to an end? "I wonder how many miles I've fallen by this time?" she said aloud. "I must be getting somewhere near the centre of the earth. Let me see: that would be four thousand miles down, I think—" (for, you see, Alice had learnt several things of this sort in her lessons in the school-room, and though this was not a *very* good opportunity for showing off her knowledge, as there was no one to listen to her, still it was good practice to say it over) "—yes, that's about the right distance—but then I wonder what Latitude or Longitude I've got to?" (Alice had not the slightest idea what Latitude was, or Longitude either, but she thought they were nice grand words to say.)

Presently she began again. "I wonder if I shall fall right *through* the earth! How funny it'll seem to come out among the people that walk with their heads downwards! The antipathies, I think—" (she was rather glad there *was* no one listening, this time, as it didn't sound at all the right word) "—but I shall have to ask them what the name of the country is, you know. Please, Ma'am, is this New Zealand? Or Australia?" (and she tried to curtsey as she spoke—fancy, *curtseying* as you're falling through the air! Do you think you could manage it?) "And what an ignorant little girl she'll think me for asking! No, it'll never do to ask: perhaps I shall see it written up somewhere."

Down, down, down. There was nothing else to do, so Alice soon began talking again. "Dinah'll miss me very much to-night, I should think!" (Dinah was the cat.) "I hope they'll remember her saucer of milk at tea-time. Dinah, my dear! I wish you were down here with me! There are no mice in the air, I'm afraid, but you might catch a bat, and that's very like a mouse, you know. But do cats eat bats, I wonder?" And here Alice began to get rather sleepy, and went on saying to herself, in a dreamy

sort of way, "Do cats eat bats? Do cats eat bats?" and
sometimes "Do bats eat cats?", for, you see, as she
couldn't answer either question, it didn't much matter
which way she put it. She felt that she was dozing off, and
had just begun to dream that she was walking hand in
hand with Dinah, and was saying to her, very earnestly,
"Now, Dinah, tell me the truth: did you ever eat a bat?",
when suddenly, thump! thump! down she came upon a
heap of sticks and dry leaves, and the fall was over.

Alice was not a bit hurt, and she jumped up on to her
feet in a moment: she looked up, but it was all dark
overhead: before her was another long passage, and the
White Rabbit was still in sight, hurrying down it. There
was not a moment to be lost: away went Alice like the
wind, and was just in time to hear it say, as it turned a
corner, "Oh my ears and whiskers, how late it's getting!"
She was close behind it when she turned the corner, but
the Rabbit was no longer to be seen: she found herself in a
long, low hall, which was lit up by a row of lamps
hanging from the roof.

There were doors all round the hall, but they were all
locked; and when Alice had been all the way down one
side and up the other, trying every door, she walked sadly
down the middle, wondering how she was ever to get out
again.

Suddenly she came upon a little three-legged table, all
made of solid glass: there was nothing on it but a tiny
golden key, and Alice's first idea was that this might
belong to one of the doors of the hall; but, alas! either the
locks were too large, or the key was too small, but at any
rate it would not open any of them. However, on the
second time round, she came upon a low curtain she had
not noticed before, and behind it was a little door about
fifteen inches high: she tried the little golden key in the
lock, and to her great delight it fitted!

Alice opened the door and found that it led into a
small passage, not much larger than a rat-hole: she knelt
down and looked along the passage into the loveliest
garden you ever saw. How she longed to get out of that
dark hall, and wander about among those beds of bright
flowers and those cool fountains, but she could not even

get her head through the doorway; "and even if my head
would go through," thought poor Alice, "it would be of
very little use without my shoulders. Oh, how I wish I
could shut up like a telescope! I think I could, if I only
knew how to begin." For, you see, so many out-of-the-way
things had happened lately, that Alice had begun to think
that very few things indeed were really impossible.

There seemed to be no use in waiting by the little
door, so she went back to the table, half hoping she might
find another key on it, or at any rate a book of rules for
shutting people up like telescopes: this time she found a
little bottle on it ("which certainly was not here before,"
said Alice), and tied round the neck of the bottle was a
paper label, with the words "DRINK ME" beautifully
printed on it in large letters.

It was all very well to say "Drink me," but the wise
little Alice was not going to do *that* in a hurry. "No, I'll

look first," she said, "and see whether it's marked *'poison'* or not"; for she had read several nice little stories about children who had got burnt, and eaten up by wild beasts, and other unpleasant things, all because they *would* not remember the simple rules their friends had taught them: such as, that a red-hot poker will burn you if you hold it too long; and that, if you cut your finger *very* deeply with a knife, it usually bleeds; and she had never forgotten that, if you drink much from a bottle marked "poison," it is almost certain to disagree with you, sooner or later.

However, this bottle was *not* marked "poison," so Alice ventured to taste it, and, finding it very nice (it had, in fact, a sort of mixed flavour of cherry-tart, custard, pineapple, roast turkey, toffy, and hot buttered toast), she very soon finished it off.

"What a curious feeling!" said Alice. "I must be shutting up like a telescope!"

And so it was indeed: she was now only ten inches high, and her face brightened up at the thought that she was now the right size for going through the little door into that lovely garden. First, however, she waited for a few minutes to see if she was going to shrink any further: she felt a little nervous about this; "for it might end, you know," said Alice to herself, "in my going out altogether, like a candle. I wonder what I should be like then?" And she tried to fancy what the flame of a candle looks like after the candle is blown out, for she could not remember ever having seen such a thing.

After a while, finding that nothing more happened, she decided on going into the garden at once; but, alas for poor Alice! when she got to the door, she found she had forgotten the little golden key, and when she went back to the table for it, she found she could not possibly reach it: she could see it quite plainly through the glass, and she tried her best to climb up one of the legs of the table, but it was too slippery; and when she had tired herself out with trying, the poor little thing sat down and cried.

"Come, there's no use in crying like that!" said Alice to herself rather sharply. "I advise you to leave off this minute!" She generally gave herself very good advice (though she very seldom followed it), and sometimes she scolded herself so severely as to bring tears into her eyes; and once she remembered trying to box her own ears for having cheated herself in a game of croquet she was playing against herself, for this curious child was very fond of pretending to be two people. "But it's no use now," thought poor Alice, "to pretend to be two people! Why, there's hardly enough of me left to make *one* respectable person!"

Soon her eye fell on a little glass box that was lying under the table: she opened it, and found in it a very small cake, on which the words "EAT ME" were beautifully marked in currants. "Well, I'll eat it," said Alice, "and if it makes me grow larger, I can reach the key; and if it makes me grow smaller, I can creep under the door: so either way I'll get into the garden, and I don't care which happens!"

She ate a little bit, and said anxiously to herself "Which way? Which way?", holding her hand on the top of her head to feel which way it was growing; and she was quite surprised to find that she remained the same size. To be sure, this is what generally happens when one eats cake; but Alice had got so much into the way of expecting nothing but out-of-the-way things to happen, that it seemed quite dull and stupid for life to go on in the common way.

So she set to work, and very soon finished off the cake.

A Strange Sled Race

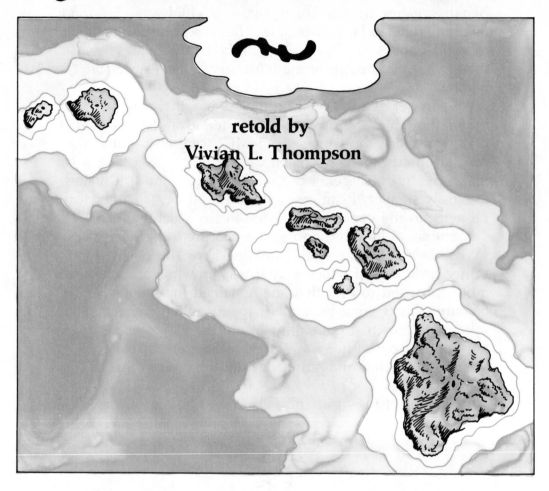

retold by
Vivian L. Thompson

Far out in the blue Pacific, a volcanic mountain range rises from the ocean floor to form the group of islands called Hawaii. Long, long ago, the Polynesians, which means "people from many islands," came to Hawaii in great double boats. They called this place "Hawaii-with-the-green-back." It was warmed by tropic sun, cooled by trade winds, washed by misty rains.

The Polynesians made these islands their new home. Mild evenings, by the light of the candlenut torches, they gathered to listen to their storytellers.

At first they heard only the stories brought from their former island homes. But in time the Hawaiians began to tell stories

about their new home, to explain the natural wonders they found
there. One story tells of the goddess of snow, Poliahu, who lives
high on the slopes of Mauna Kea on the northern side of Hawaii.
That side is free of lava flows because of the goddess's skill at sled
racing.

Poliahu and her snow maidens one day covered their
dazzling snow mantles with mantles of golden sunshine.
They took their long, slender sleds to the race course
below the snowfields. There a narrow, grassy track had
been laid, dropping swiftly toward the sea.

High, tinkling laughter filled the air as the maidens
urged the goddess to race. Poliahu was very willing. She
made a running start, threw herself upon her sled, and
plunged down. Far below she came to a stop, marked the
spot, and lifted her sled aside.

One after another the snow maidens followed, but
none reached the goddess's mark. As they gathered below
they discovered a stranger in their midst, a handsome
woman dressed in black mantle and robe.

Fixing gleaming black eyes upon the goddess of snow,
she spoke. "I should like to race with you, but I have no
sled."

"You may use one of ours," Snow Goddess said, and
a maiden quickly offered hers.

The stranger took it without a word of thanks. Then
she and Poliahu climbed up the mountain slope. The
maidens watched from below. The stranger swooped down
the slope and flashed past them. There was no doubt she
was skillful. Poliahu followed and passed the other's
stopping place.

"That sled did not fit me!" said the dark-eyed stranger.

A taller maiden offered her sled. Again the long, slow
climb. Again the short, swift descent. Both sleds went
farther than before, but Poliahu's still led.

"An inferior sled!" the woman said with scorn.

"We have no inferior sleds," Snow Goddess replied
coldly. "Let us race again, and you shall take mine."

"I have always raced on a longer course," said the
woman. "Let us go higher up the mountain. You shall race
first this time."

They exchanged sleds and climbed to the snow line.
The stranger waited until Poliahu had started down; then
she stamped her foot. The earth trembled. A jagged crack
split open across the lower part of the racing course.

The snow maidens, watching below, lost sight of their
goddess as steam rose from the crack and formed a
curtain. They ran up the slope.

For a moment, the steam cleared. They caught a glimpse of Poliahu racing toward the widening crack. The woman in black was close behind her, standing upright on her speeding sled. In horror they saw her black robe turn red and her eyes glow like burning coals. They knew now! She was Pele—Volcano Goddess!

She stamped again. They felt the molten lava come rumbling through underground passages in answer to her signal. It spurted out along the crack.

Swiftly the snow maidens raised their arms toward the snowy peaks and began to chant. The air grew chill as gray cloud goddesses gathered to aid Poliahu. They sent snow swirling down from the top of the mountain, hissing as it struck the heated earth. The spurting lava died.

Pele, in a fury, gave a crackling shout. The lava leaped up again, forming a row of fiery fountains directly ahead of Poliahu.

The snow maidens watched fearfully. There was no way that Poliahu could slow her sled nor turn it aside. She plunged through the wall of fire.

Her golden mantle burst into flame. Throwing it off and leaping from her sled, Snow Goddess stood robed in dazzling white. A red-gold river raced toward her from the fire fountains. On its crest rode Pele. Poliahu waited, unmoved.

Volcano Goddess burst through the flames without harm. She sprang from her sled to face the young woman who dared to defy her.

Snow Goddess swung her mantle in a wide arc. A blast of icy wind swept down the mountain. Her silvery hair and dazzling garments streamed out behind her.

Volcano Goddess shivered. The leaping fountains dwindled. The racing river slowed.

She screamed at the lava, "Swallow her up!"

But the lava fountains died. The lava river grew sluggish. Still deadly, it flowed to the very feet of Snow Goddess. She flung her arms wide. The river split in two, leaving her unharmed in the center. It made its way beyond her, moving slowly down to the sea. There it formed a long, flat point of land, known to this day as Leaf-of-Smooth-Lava.

Volcano Goddess stared, unable to believe what she saw. Her red mantle turned black again. Her glowing eyes dulled. Shivering with cold, she disappeared as mysteriously as she had come.

High, tinkling laughter filled the air once more as the snow goddess and her maidens picked up their sleds and returned to their snowy home.

Pele never again crossed over Mauna Kea to Poliahu's side of the island, although she still sent lava pouring down the southern side.

excerpt from

Jennifer, Hecate, Macbeth, William McKinley, and Me, Elizabeth

E. L. Konigsburg

I first met Jennifer on my way to school. It was Halloween, and she was sitting in a tree. I was going back to school from lunch. This particular lunch hour was only a little different from usual because of Halloween. We were told to dress in costume for the school Halloween parade. I was dressed as a Pilgrim.

I always walked the back road to school, and I always walked alone. We had moved to the apartment house in town in September just before school started, and I walked alone because I didn't have anyone to walk with. I walked the back way because I passed through a little woods that I liked. Jennifer was sitting in one of the trees in this woods.

Our apartment house had grown on a farm about ten years before. There was still a small farm across the street; it included a big white house, a greenhouse, a caretaker's house, and a pump painted green without a handle. The greenhouse had clean windows; they shone in the sun. I could see only the roof windows from our second floor apartment. The rest were hidden by trees and shrubs. My mother never called the place a farm; she always called it THE ESTATE. It was old; the lady who owned it was old. She had given part of her land to the town for a park, and the town named the park after her: Samellson Park. THE ESTATE gave us a beautiful view from our apartment. My mother liked trees.

Our new town was not full of apartments. Almost everyone else lived in houses. There were only three apartment buildings as big as ours. All three sat on the top of the hill from the train station. Hundreds of men rode the train to New York City every morning and rode it home every night. My father did. In the mornings the elevators would be full of kids going to school and fathers going to the train. The kids left the building by the back door and ran down one side of the hill to the school. The fathers left the building by the front door and ran down the other side of the hill to the station.

Other kids from the apartment chose to walk to school through the little woods. The footsteps of all of them for ten years had worn away the soil so that the roots of the trees were bare and made steps for walking up and down the steep slope. The little woods made better company than the sidewalks. I liked the smells of the trees and the colors of the trees. I liked to walk with my head way up, practically hanging over my back. Then I could see the patterns the leaves formed against the blue sky.

I had my head way back and was watching the leaves when I first saw Jennifer up in the tree. She was dressed as a Pilgrim, too. I saw her feet first. She was sitting on one of the lower branches of the tree swinging her feet. That's how I happened to see her feet first. They were just about the boniest feet I had ever seen. Swinging right in front of my eyes as if I were sitting in the first row at Cinerama. They wore real Pilgrim shoes make of buckles and cracked old leather. The heel part flapped up and down because the shoes were so big that only the toe part could stay attached. Those shoes looked as if they were going to fall off any minute.

I grabbed the heel of the shoe and shoved it back onto the heel of that bony foot. Then I wiped my hands on my Pilgrim apron and looked up at Jennifer. I didn't know yet that she was Jennifer. She was not smiling, and I was embarrassed.

I said in a loud voice, which I hoped would sound stout red but which came out sounding thin blue, "You're going to lose that shoe."

The first thing Jennifer ever said to me was, "Witches never lose anything."

"But you're not a witch," I said. "You're a Pilgrim, and look, so am I."

"I won't argue with you," she said. "Witches convince; they never argue. But I'll tell you this much. Real witches are Pilgrims, and just because I don't have on a silly black costume and carry a silly broom and wear a silly black hat, doesn't mean that I'm not a witch. I'm a witch all the time and not just on Halloween."

I didn't know what to say, so I said what my mother always says when she can't answer one of my questions. I said, "You better hurry up now, or you'll be late for school."

"Witches are never late," she said.

"But witches have to go to school." I wished I had said something clever.

"I just go to school because I'm putting the teacher under a spell," she said.

"Which teacher?" I asked. "Get it? *Witch* teacher?" I laughed. I was pleased that now I had said something clever.

Jennifer neither laughed nor answered. But I was sure she'd got it. She looked at me hard and said, "Give me those three chocolate chip cookies, and I'll come down and tell you my name, and I'll walk the rest of the way to school with you."

I wasn't particularly hungry for the cookies, but I was hungry for company, so I said, "Okay," and reached out my hand holding the cookies. I wondered how she could tell that they were chocolate chips. They were in a bag.

As she began to swing down from the branches, I caught a glimpse of her underwear. I expected that it would look dusty, and it did. But that was not why it was not like any underwear I had ever seen. It was old fashioned. There were buttons and no elastic. She also had on yards and yards of petticoats. Her Pilgrim dress looked older than mine. Much older. Much, much older. Hers looked ancient. Of course, my Pilgrim costume was not new either. I had worn it the year before, but then I had been in a different grade in a different school. My cousin had worn the costume before that. I hadn't grown much during the year. My dress was only a little short, and only a little tight, and only a little scratchy where it was pinned, and it was only absolutely uncomfortable. In other words, my costume was a hand-me-down, but Jennifer's was a genuine antique.

After Jennifer touched the ground, I saw that she was taller than I. Everybody was. I was the shortest kid in my class. I was always the shortest kid in my class. She was thin. Skinny is what she really was. She came toward my hand and looked hard at the bag of cookies.

"Are you sure you didn't bite any of them?" she demanded.

"Sure I'm sure," I said. I was getting mad, but a bargain's a bargain.

"Well," she said, taking one cookie out of the bag, "My name is Jennifer. Now let's get going." As she said "going," she grabbed the bag with the other two cookies and started to walk.

"Wait up," I yelled. "A bargain's a bargain. Don't you want to know my name?"

"I told you witches are never late, but I can't be responsible for you yet . . . Elizabeth."

She knew my name already! She walked so fast that I was almost convinced that she was a witch; she was practically flying. We got to school just as the tardy bell began to ring. Jennifer's room was a fifth grade just off the corridor near the entrance, and she slipped into her classroom while the bell was still buzzing. My room was four doors further down the hall, and I got to my room *after* the bell had stopped.

She had said that witches are never late. Being late felt as uncomfortable as my tight Pilgrim dress. No Pilgrim had ever suffered as much as I did. Walking to my seat while everyone stared at me was awful. My desk was in the back of the room; it was a long, long walk. The whole class had time to see that I was a blushing Pilgrim. I knew that I was ready to cry. The whole class didn't have to know that too, so I didn't raise my eyes until I was seated and felt sure that they wouldn't leak. When I looked up, I saw that there were six Pilgrims: three other Pilgrim girls and two Pilgrim boys. That's a lot of Pilgrims for a class of twenty. But none of them could be witches, I thought. After checking over their costumes and shoes, I decided that at least three of them had cousins who had been Pilgrims the year before.

Miss Hazen announced that she would postpone my detention until the next day because of the Halloween parade. Detention was a school rule; if you were late coming to school, you stayed after school that day. The kids called it "staying after." I didn't feel grateful for the postponement. She could have skipped my "staying after" altogether.

Our lesson that afternoon was short, and I didn't perform too well. I had to tug on my dress a lot and scratch under my Pilgrim hat a lot. I would have scratched other places where the costume itched, but they weren't polite.

At last we were all lined up in the hall. Each class was to march to the auditorium and be seated. Then one class at a time would walk across the stage before the judges. The rest of the classes would be the audience. The classes at the end of the hall marched to the auditorium first.

There were classes on both sides of the hall near my room, and the space for the marchers was narrow. Some of the children had large cardboard cartons over them and were supposed to be packages of cigarettes or sports cars. These costumes had trouble getting through. Then there was Jennifer. She was last in line. She looked neither to the right nor to the left but slightly up toward the ceiling. I kept my eye on her hoping she'd say "Hi" so that I wouldn't feel so alone standing there. She didn't. Instead, well, I almost didn't believe what I actually saw her do.

But before I tell what I saw her do, I have to tell about Cynthia. Every grown-up in the whole U.S. of A. thinks that Cynthia is perfect. She is pretty and neat and smart. I guess that makes perfect to almost any grown-up. Since she lives in the same apartment house as we do, and since my mother is a grown-up, and since my mother thinks that she is perfect, my mother had tried hard to have us become friends since we first moved to town. My mother would drop hints. HINT: Why don't you call Cynthia and ask her if she would like to show you where the library is? Then you can both eat lunch here. Or HINT: Why don't you run over and play with Cynthia while I unpack the groceries?

It didn't take me long to discover that what Cynthia was, was not perfect. The word for what Cynthia was, was *mean*.

Here's an example of mean. There was a little boy in our building who had moved in about a month before we did. His name was Johann; that's German for John. He moved from Germany and didn't speak English yet. He loved Cynthia. Because she was so pretty, I guess. He followed her around and said, "Cynsssia, Cynsssia." Cynthia always made fun of him. She would stick her tongue between her teeth and say, "Th, th, th, th, th. My name is Cyn-*th*-ia not Cyn-*sss*-ia." Johann would smile and say, "Cyn-*sss*-ia." Cynthia would stick out her tongue and say "Th, th, th, th, th." And then she'd walk away from him. I liked Johann. I wished he would follow me around. I would have taught him English, and I would never even have minded if he called me Elizabessss. Another word for what Cynthia was, was *two-faced*. Because every time some grown-up was around, she was sweet to Johann. She'd smile at him and pat his head . . . only until the grown-up left.

And another thing: Cynthia certainly didn't need me for a friend. She had a very good friend called Dolores who also lived in the apartment house. They told secrets and giggled together whenever I got into the elevator with them. So I got into the habit of leaving for school before they did. Sometimes, on weekends, they'd be in the elevator when I got on; I'd act as if they weren't there. I had to get off the elevator before they did because I lived on the second floor, and they lived on the sixth. Before I'd get off the elevator, I'd take my fists, and fast and furious, I'd push every floor button just the second before I got out. I'd step out of the elevator and watch the dial stopping at every floor on the way up. Then I'd skip home to our apartment.

For Halloween Cynthia wore everything real ballerinas wear: leotards and tights and ballet slippers and a tutu. A tutu is a little short skirt that ballerinas wear somewhere around their waists. Hers looked like a nylon net doughnut floating around her middle. Besides all the equipment I listed above, Cynthia wore rouge and eye make-up and lipstick and a tiara. She looked glamorous, but I could tell that she felt plenty chilly in that costume. Her teeth were chattering. She wouldn't put on a sweater.

As we were standing in the hall waiting for our turn to go to the auditorium, and as Jennifer's class passed, Cynthia was turned around talking to Dolores. Dolores was dressed as a Pilgrim. They were both whispering and giggling. Probably about Jennifer.

Here's what Jennifer did. As she passed Cynthia, she reached out and quicker than a blink unsnapped the tutu. I happened to be watching her closely, but even I didn't believe that she had really done it. Jennifer clop-clopped along in the line with her eyes still up toward the ceiling and passed me a note almost without my knowing. She did it so fast that I wasn't even sure she did it until I felt the note in my hand and crunched it beneath my apron to hide it. Jennifer never took her eyes off the ceiling or broke out of line for even half a step.

I wanted to make sure that everyone saw Cynthia with her tutu down, so I pointed my finger at her and said, "O-o-o-o-oh!" I said it loud. Of course, that made everyone on both sides of the aisle notice her and start to giggle.

Cynthia didn't have sense enough to be embarrassed. She loved attention so much that she didn't care if her tutu had fallen. She stepped out of it, picked it up, shook it out, floated it over her head, and anchored it back around her waist. She touched her hands to her hair, giving it little pushes the way women do who have just come out of the beauty parlor. I hoped she was itchy.

Finally, our class got to the auditorium. After I sat down, I opened the note, holding both my hands under my Pilgrim apron. I slowly slipped my hands out and glanced at the note. I was amazed at what I saw. Jennifer's note looked like this:

> *Meet for Trick or Treat at Half after six P.M. o'clock of this evening. By the same tree. Bring two (2) bags. Those were good cookies.*

I studied the note a long time. I thought about the note as I watched the Halloween parade; I wondered if Jennifer used a quill pen. You can guess that I didn't win any prizes for my costume. Neither did Cynthia. Neither did Jennifer (even though I thought she should have). We all marched across the stage wearing our masks and stopped for a curtsy or bow (depending on whether you were a girl or a boy) in front of the judges who were sitting at a table in the middle of the stage. Some of the girls who were disguised as boys forgot themselves and curtsied. Then we marched off. Our class was still seated when Jennifer clop-clopped across the stage in those crazy Pilgrim slippers. She didn't wear a mask at all. She wore a big brown paper bag over her head and *there were no holes cut out for her eyes.* Yet, she walked up the stairs, across the stage, stopped and curtsied, and walked off without tripping or falling or walking out of those gigantic shoes.

The Lion, the Witch and the Wardrobe

C. S. Lewis

Lucy Looks into a Wardrobe

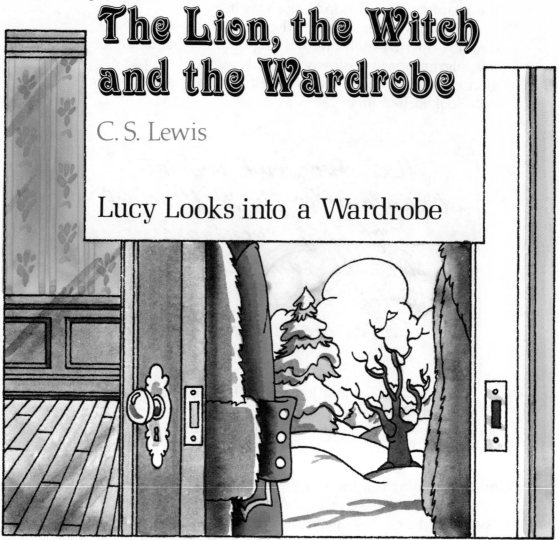

The Lion, the Witch and the Wardrobe *tells of four children who visit an enchanted land that is reached through a wardrobe, or closet, in a large house in England. This chapter tells how one of the children accidentally discovers the land of Narnia.*

Once there were four children whose names were Peter, Susan, Edmund and Lucy. This story is about something that happened to them when they were sent away from London during the war because of the air-raids. They were sent to the house of an old Professor who lived in the heart of the country, ten miles from the nearest railway station and two miles from the nearest post office. He had no wife and he lived in a very large house with a housekeeper called Mrs. Macready and three servants. (Their names were Ivy, Margaret and Betty, but they do not come into the story much.) He himself was a very old man with shaggy white hair, which grew over most of his face as well as on his head, and they liked him almost at once; but on the first evening when he came out to meet them at the front door he was so odd-looking that Lucy (who was the youngest) was a little afraid of him, and Edmund (who was the next youngest) wanted to laugh and had to keep on pretending he was blowing his nose to hide it.

As soon as they had said good night to the Professor and gone upstairs on the first night, the boys came into the girls' room and they all talked it over.

"We've fallen on our feet and no mistake," said Peter. "This is going to be perfectly splendid. That old chap will let us do anything we like."

"I think he's an old dear," said Susan.

"Oh, come off it!" said Edmund, who was tired and pretending not to be tired, which always made him bad-tempered. "Don't go on talking like that."

"Like what?" said Susan; "and anyway, it's time you were in bed."

"Trying to talk like Mother," said Edmund. "And who are you to say when I'm to go to bed? Go to bed yourself."

"Hadn't we all better go to bed?" said Lucy. "There's sure to be a row if we're heard talking here."

"No there won't," said Peter. "I tell you this is the sort of house where no one's going to mind what we do. Anyway, they won't hear us. It's about ten minutes' walk from here down to that dining room, and any amount of stairs and passages in between."

"What's that noise?" said Lucy suddenly. It was a far larger house than she had ever been in before and the thought of all those long passages and rows of doors leading into empty rooms was beginning to make her feel a little creepy.

"It's only a bird, silly," said Edmund.

"It's an owl," said Peter. "This is going to be a wonderful place for birds. I shall go to bed now. I say, let's go and explore to-morrow. You might find anything in a place like this. Did you see those mountains as we came along? And the woods? There might be eagles. There might be stags. There'll be hawks."

"Badgers!" said Lucy.

"Snakes!" said Edmund.

"Foxes!" said Susan.

But when next morning came, there was a steady rain falling, so thick that when you looked out of the window you could see neither the mountains nor the woods nor even the stream in the garden.

"Of course it _would_ be raining!" said Edmund. They had just finished breakfast with the Professor and were upstairs in the room he had set apart for them—a long, low room with two windows looking out in one direction and two in another.

"Do stop grumbling, Ed," said Susan. "Ten to one it'll clear up in an hour or so. And in the meantime we're pretty well off. There's a wireless and lots of books."

"Not for me," said Peter, "I'm going to explore in the house."

Everyone agreed to this and that was how the adventures began. It was the sort of house that you never seem to come to the end of, and it was full of unexpected places. The first few doors they tried led only into spare bedrooms, as everyone had expected that they would; but soon they came to a very long room full of pictures and there they found a suit of armour; and after that was a room all hung with green, with a harp in one corner; and then came three steps down and five steps up, and then a kind of little upstairs hall and a door that led out onto a balcony, and then a whole series of rooms that led into each other and were lined with books—most of them very old books and some bigger than a Bible in a church. And shortly after that they looked into a room that was quite empty except for one big wardrobe; the sort that has a looking-glass in the door. There was nothing else in the room at all except a dead blue-bottle on the window-sill.

"Nothing there!" said Peter, and they all trooped out again—all except Lucy. She stayed behind because she thought it would be worth while trying the door of the wardrobe, even though she felt almost sure that it would be locked. To her surprise it opened quite easily, and two moth-balls dropped out.

Looking into the inside, she saw several coats hanging up—mostly long fur coats. There was nothing Lucy liked so much as the smell and feel of fur. She immediately stepped into the wardrobe and got in among the coats and rubbed her face against them, leaving the door open, of course, because she knew that it is very foolish to shut oneself into any wardrobe. Soon she went further in and found that there was a second row of coats hanging up behind the first one. It was almost quite dark in there and she kept her arms stretched out in front of her so as not to bump her face into the back of the wardrobe. She took a step further in—then two or three steps—always expecting to feel woodwork against the tips of her fingers. But she could not feel it.

"This must be a simply enormous wardrobe!" thought Lucy, going still further in and pushing the soft folds of the coats aside to make room for her. Then she noticed that there was something crunching under her feet. "I wonder is that more moth-balls?" she thought, stooping down to feel it with her hands. But instead of feeling the hard, smooth wood of the floor of the wardrobe, she felt something soft and powdery and extremely cold. "This is very queer," she said, and went on a step or two further.

Next moment she found that what was rubbing against her face and hands was no longer soft fur but something hard and rough and even prickly. "Why, it is just like branches of trees!" exclaimed Lucy. And then she saw that there was a light ahead of her; not a few inches away where the back of the wardrobe ought to have been, but a long way off. Something cold and soft was falling on her. A moment later she found that she was standing in the middle of a wood at night-time with snow under her feet and snowflakes falling through the air.

Lucy felt a little frightened, but she felt very inquisitive and excited as well. She looked back over her shoulder and there, between the dark tree-trunks, she could still see the open doorway of the wardrobe and even catch a glimpse of the empty room from which she had set out. (She had, of course, left the door open, for she knew that it is a very silly thing to shut oneself into a wardrobe.) It seemed to be still daylight there. "I can always get back if anything goes wrong," thought Lucy. She began to walk forward, *crunch-crunch*, over the snow and through the wood towards the other light.

In about ten minutes she reached it and found that it was a lamp-post. As she stood looking at it, wondering why there was a lamp-post in the middle of a wood and wondering what to do next, she heard a pitter patter of feet coming towards her. And soon after that a very strange person stepped out from among the trees into the light of the lamp-post.

He was only a little taller than Lucy herself and he carried over his head an umbrella, white with snow. From the waist upwards he was like a man, but his legs were shaped like a goat's (the hair on them was glossy black) and instead of feet he had goat's hoofs. He also had a tail, but Lucy did not notice this at first because it was neatly caught up over the arm that held the umbrella so as to keep it from trailing in the snow. He had a red woollen muffler round his neck and his skin was rather reddish too. He had a strange, but pleasant little face with a short pointed beard and curly hair, and out of the hair there stuck two horns, one on each side of his forehead. One of his hands, as I have said, held the umbrella: in the other arm he carried several brown paper parcels. What with the parcels and the snow it looked just as if he had been doing his Christmas shopping. He was a Faun. And when he saw Lucy he gave such a start of surprise that he dropped all his parcels.

"Goodness gracious me!" exclaimed the Faun.

THINGS FALL APART

Chinua Achebe

Low voices, broken now and again by singing, reached
Okonkwo from his wives' huts as each woman and her
children told folk stories. Ekwefi and her daughter,
Ezinma, sat on a mat on the floor. It was Ekwefi's turn to
tell a story.

"Once upon a time," she began, "all the birds were
invited to a feast in the sky. They were very happy and
began to prepare themselves for the great day. They
painted their bodies with red cam wood and drew beautiful
patterns on them with dye.

"Tortoise saw all these preparations and soon
discovered what it all meant. Nothing that happened in the
world of the animals ever escaped his notice; he was full of
cunning. As soon as he heard of the great feast in the sky
his throat began to itch at the very thought. There was a
famine in those days and Tortoise had not eaten a good
meal for two moons. His body rattled like a piece of dry
stick in his empty shell. So he began to plan how he
would go to the sky."

"But he had no wings," said Ezinma.

"Be patient," replied her mother. "That is the story.
Tortoise had no wings, but he went to the birds and asked
to be allowed to go with them.

" 'We know you too well,' said the birds when they had heard him. 'You are full of cunning and you are ungrateful. If we allow you to come with us you will soon begin your mischief.'

" 'You do not know me,' said Tortoise. 'I am a changed man. I have learned that a man who makes trouble for others is also making it for himself.'

"Tortoise had a sweet tongue, and within a short time all the birds agreed that he was a changed man, and they each gave him a feather, with which he made two wings.

"At last the great day came and Tortoise was the first to arrive at the meeting place. When all the birds had gathered together, they set off in a body. Tortoise was very happy as he flew among the birds, and he was soon chosen as the man to speak for the party because he was a great orator.

" 'There is one important thing which we must not forget,' he said as they flew on their way. 'When people are invited to a great feast like this, they take new names for the occasion. Our hosts in the sky will expect us to honor this age-old custom.'

"None of the birds had heard of this custom but they knew that Tortoise, in spite of his failings in other directions, was a widely traveled man who knew the customs of different peoples. And so they each took a new name. When they had all taken, Tortoise also took one. He was to be called *All of you*.

"At last the party arrived in the sky and their hosts were very happy to see them. Tortoise stood up in his many-colored plumage and thanked them for their invitation. His speech was so eloquent that all the birds were glad they had brought him, and nodded their heads in approval of all he said. Their hosts took him as the king of the birds, especially as he looked somewhat different from the others.

"After kola nuts had been presented and eaten, the people of the sky set before their guests the most delectable dishes Tortoise had even seen or dreamed of. The soup was brought out hot from the fire and in the very pot in which it had been cooked. It was full of meat and fish. Tortoise began to sniff aloud. There was pounded yam and also yam pottage cooked with palm oil and fresh fish. There were also pots of palm wine. When everything had been set before the guests, one of the people of the sky came forward and tasted a little from each pot. He then invited the birds to eat. But Tortoise jumped to his feet and asked: 'For whom have you prepared this feast?'

" 'For all of you,' replied the man.

"Tortoise turned to the birds and said: 'You remember that my name is *All of you*. The custom here is to serve the spokesman first and the others later. They will serve you when I have eaten.'

"He began to eat and the birds grumbled angrily. The people of the sky thought it must be their custom to leave all the food for their king. And so Tortoise ate the best part of the food and then drank two pots of palm wine, so that he was full of food and drink and his body grew fat enough to fill out his shell.

"The birds gathered round to eat what was left and to peck at the bones he had thrown all about the floor. Some of them were too angry to eat. They chose to fly home on an empty stomach. But before they left each took back the feather he had lent to Tortoise. And there he stood in his hard shell full of food and wine but without any wings to fly home. He asked the birds to take a message for his wife, but they all refused. In the end Parrot, who had felt more angry than the others, suddenly changed his mind and agreed to take the message.

" 'Tell my wife,' said Tortoise, 'to bring out all the soft things in my house and cover the compound with them so that I can jump down from the sky without very great danger.'

"Parrot promised to deliver the message, and then flew away. But when he reached Tortoise's house he told his wife to bring out all the hard things in the house. And so she brought out her husband's hoes, machetes, spears, guns, and even his cannon. Tortoise looked down from the sky and saw his wife bringing things out, but it was too far to see what they were. When all seemed ready he let himself go. He fell and fell and fell until he began to fear that he would never stop falling. And then like the sound of his cannon he crashed on the compound."

"Did he die?" asked Ezinma.

"No," replied Ekwefi. "His shell broke into pieces. But there was a great medicine man in the neighborhood. Tortoise's wife sent for him and he gathered all the bits of shell and stuck them together. That is why Tortoise's shell is not smooth."

ZOO 2000

Richard Curtis

Steven Barber tugged his father's hand. "Can we look at something else? This one isn't so interesting."

In a spacious cage before them the great cat lay dozing on a concrete slab, tail and ears languidly switching and twitching away flies. After the South American jaguar, which they'd watched tearing a slab of beef to shreds in the adjoining cage, the sight of a sleeping lion was a decided letdown. Besides, the musky odor of cats had begun to oppress Steven.

But his father resisted the tug and stood studying the plaque on the guard rail. "Just a moment. Did you read this?"

"No," the boy said with a sigh.

"According to it, the African lion was a brownish-orange color until well into the twenty-first century."

Steven looked at the dormant beast. "How did it get to be gray?"

Mr. Barber finished reading. "The same way all the other creatures were transformed."

"The Great Mutation, right?"

"Right."

His son nodded, then shrugged. It was hard to see what difference it made. A sleeping gray lion was just as boring as a sleeping brownish-orange one.

"I wish he'd get up and do something," Steven said with a whine, throwing a peanut at the lion. It landed on the beast's sleek gray flank. The lion's muscle rippled, but it would take a considerably greater provocation than that to arouse him.

"I wish you'd leave the animals alone," his father said sternly. "How'd you like it if someone threw peanuts at *you* while you were trying to sleep?" He reached for the bag, but Steven promised he wouldn't do it anymore, and Mr. Barber relented.

They passed on to the next cage. "Is that the color lions used to be?"

Mr. Barber peered at the lithe orangey-brown cat pacing rapidly between the walls of his cage, snarling nastily. "This is a leopard," he said, stooping over to examine the plaque. "I would say the lion was that color, yes." He read the text. "Hmmm, that's interesting."

"What is?"

"Leopards used to have spots. Little black rings."

"What for?"

"Camouflage. The spots helped them blend into the shadows of the bush."

"Did leopards lose their spots in The Great Mutation, too?"

"Yes. And that is why they're nearly extinct. With their natural protective coloring gone, it became harder for them to stalk their prey or hide from hunters."

Steven closed his eyes momentarily and imagined himself a hunter. What must it be like to sight down a rifle barrel as hundreds of pounds of fanged death charge and leap? A shiver wracked him and, noting that his father was still absorbed in the plaque, he flicked a peanut at the leopard. The missile grazed its muzzle and it uttered a chilling roar.

"Let's go," the boy said. He looked nervously over his shoulder as they moved towards the doors of the lion house.

They strolled across the promenade in the warm spring air in the direction of a clamor of snorts, honks, splashes, and children's laughter. Just beyond the hedgerow, they saw the seal pool. It was encircled six deep by a crowd of parents and children.

They took a place on the periphery and waited for people to leave so that they could progress to the rail. While they stood with vision blocked, Steven asked, "What exactly was The Great Mutation? I mean, I know it changed a lot of things, but . . ."

"It changed everything," his father said dramatically. "It was probably the most significant event in the history of this planet since the passing of the Ice Age."

"But I still don't know what really happened, except that it had to do with radiation. Does that mean an atomic bomb?"

"No, it was a different form of atomic energy. You see, in the last third of the twentieth century, men built hundreds of nuclear power plants to generate electricity. There was much opposition to them. Many people felt that they produced dangerous radiation. But still the world needed power, needed electricity. And so the atomic plants were built."

"Why did people build them if they were so dangerous?"

"They believed that as long as the radiation was safely contained, there was no danger. And it *was* safely contained, too, for quite a while. But in the 1990s a

183

number of terrible accidents occurred, explosions and leaks that contaminated the atmosphere with radioactive gas. The radiation levels in the atmosphere reached a critical level and . . ." He looked at his son to make sure his attention hadn't wandered.

The boy had shouldered his way into a space left by a departing family. But as soon as they'd occupied it, Steven turned his face up and said, "And . . .?"

"And it began to have a bad effect on the genetic structure of practically every living thing on earth."

Steven looked at him blankly. Mr. Barber drew in a quick breath and began a brief explanation. The distinctive characteristics of the species are governed by the genes in their reproductive systems. These genes, he told his son, are extremely sensitive to radiation. And if they are sufficiently exposed to it, they can be altered. Sometimes radically. "So that a leopard, say, will be born without spots, and will pass that characteristic along to its young until the entire species is unspotted. And *that,* on a world-wide scale, is what happened. Of course it didn't happen overnight. The changes showed up in some species at once. In others, it took generations. There's another example," he said as a couple at the rail turned away, giving them an unobstructed view of the frolicking seals.

For a moment they saw nothing but streaks of silvery brown beneath the surface of the pool. Then an attendant in a green uniform bearing a large basket of fish appeared and tossed a few samples into the pool. The surface of the pool exploded with foam as seals torpedoed up to snatch their meals.

It was still impossible to see anything except an occasional snout. But as soon as the attendant stepped onto the concrete apron directly in front of Steven and his father, the seals catapulted out of the water, boosting themselves up. They were around the attendant in an instant, to the delighted murmurs of the crowd. There were six of them: a bull, three cows, and two young.

Steven watched them as they fed. They sat on their haunches, catching fish in their mouths and occasionally using their hands to hold the food, squirrel-fashion. "What did seals used to be like?" he asked.

"Certainly not like that," said his father with a laugh. He told Steven about pre-Great Mutation seals with finned tails instead of webbed hind legs, and stunted flippers instead of arms long enough to reach the mouth, with hands at the ends.

The attendant emptied his basket and left. With the highlight of the day concluded, the crowd rapidly dispersed for other attractions.

"How about the bears?" Mr. Barber suggested.

"Fine," said Steven, tossing his paper bag full of peanut shells at the bull seal when Mr. Barber turned his back. The bull waddled over to it, sniffed at it, and brushed it into the water with his nose.

The bears were kept in an outdoor setting with concrete caves and terraces, trees, and miniature ponds. The enclosure was divided into sections for each species of bear, and the whole area was surrounded by an iron fence. As an additional precaution, a moat separated the fence and the spectators' guard rail.

"Are these bears different from the twentieth-century ones?" Steven asked.

"The polar bear isn't. Nor the brown bear," Mr. Barber answered. "But this next one, the grizzly, obviously is."

They sidled up to the sub-enclosure containing the fearsome animal. This time Steven didn't have to ask what his father meant. "Wow, look at that! Three eyes!"

Once again his father was studying the plaque. "This says that in prehistoric times, many animals may have had a third eye in the middle of their foreheads. It was an extension of the pineal gland in their brains. But apparently nature decided it was unnecessary and phased it out. In the grizzly's case, though, it seems to have made a comeback. Ugh. It's not to *my* taste, I'll tell you that."

Steven watched raptly as the grizzly, head bobbing like a turtle's, sauntered up to the fence, raised itself on its hind legs, and put an imploring paw out. The little congregation of spectators backed away, then realized the bear was only begging, and returned to the guard rail. They began to throw tidbits at the bear. Steven could have kicked himself for not saving his peanuts. Then he noticed that a few morsels fell short of the cage and accumulated

185

on a ledge on the other side of the moat. Before his father could stop him, Steven had leaned across the moat and was stretching to pick up a piece of food. The grizzly's great clawed paw swooped down, grasped his hand, and yanked him clear across the mat.

Steven shrieked with pain as the bear stuffed the hand into its mouth and mauled it with powerful teeth. Several women screamed hysterically and two men rushed off calling for help.

Mr. Barber had enough presence of mind to lean over and grasp his dangling son by the legs. Another man began beating the bear on the snout with his umbrella. At last the tormented bear released Steven and helping hands pulled the boy to safety.

The next hours were a confused blur for Mr. Barber. A doctor in the crowd had torn off his shirt and improvised a bandage and tourniquet. At length an ambulance arrived. Mr. Barber barely remembered the wild ride and the emergency room of the hospital. At that point he himself had passed out.

He awoke in a darkened hospital room and for a moment could not remember why he was there. Then it came to him and he called his son's name. A nurse outside summoned a doctor and a young bearded man entered the room, blocking Mr. Barber's way.

"Please, sir, sit down. Your son is in good hands. His condition is serious but he will survive." He signaled to the nurse, who handed him a hypodermic needle. "The best thing you can do is keep calm. This will help."

Mr. Barber submitted to the needle and in a moment felt a rush of tranquilizing drug coursing through his system.

"I'm all right now. Please tell me about Steven."

The doctor's face was grave. "That hand took a terrible mauling, Mr. Barber. I'm . . . I'm afraid we had to amputate it."

"Oh, God!" Mr. Barber moaned. "Has Mrs. Barber . . .?"

"She seems to have been out all day, but we'll keep trying."

A long silence followed during which Mr. Barber struggled with his shock while the doctor struggled with his awkwardness. Then the doctor said, "There isn't much that can be said on occasions like this. But, well, it isn't the end of the world. Many people live with the loss of a hand, and of course there are excellent rehabilitation programs."

"Yes," said Mr. Barber bleakly, not really believing it.

"Also it may be of some small consolation to realize the boy still has three good hands left. We tend to forget that for a million years or so, man had to make do with only two. So Steven is still one hand ahead of the game."

"I suppose so," Mr. Barber said. "I guess we have to look at the bright side."

"That's the spirit," the doctor said cheerfully. "Now I'll take you down the hall to see your son."

———●———————●———

excerpt from

The Adventures of Pinocchio: Tale of a Puppet

C. Collodi

The story of Pinocchio was written about 100 years ago by a newspaper reporter who lived in Italy. Perhaps you have seen the cartoon movie Pinocchio. *The story tells of a wooden puppet who tries very hard to become a real boy!*

Geppetto, who was very poor, lived in a tiny basement room. The only light came through a window near the stairway outside his room. His furniture was as plain as could be: an old kitchen chair, a broken-down old bed, and a wobbly old table. At one end of his room there was a fireplace, and it had a fire burning—but the fire was just painted on the wall. Above the painted fire a painted kettle boiled merrily, sending forth a cloud of painted steam that looked quite real.

As soon as he reached the room, Geppetto got out his tools to start carving his puppet. But then he stopped to think.

"What name shall I give him?" he asked himself. "I know—I'll call him *Pinocchio*. It's a lucky name! I used to be friends with a whole family named Pinocchio: Papa Pinocchio, Mama Pinocchia, and all the little Pinocchi-kids. They made a wonderful living, that family. One of them became so rich he was a beggar!"

Now that he had found a name, Geppetto went right to work on the puppet. Very quickly he carved the hair, then the forehead, and then the eyes.

Imagine how he felt when he saw the eyes move! And then they began staring at him.

Those two staring wooden eyes gave him a creepy feeling. He hated the feeling and asked, "Nasty eyes of wood, why do you stare at me so?"

But the eyes did not answer.

Next, he made the nose! And what a nose! It kept growing as soon as he carved it. It grew and grew and grew, and in just a few minutes he began to fear it would never stop.

Poor Geppetto tired himself out trying to shorten it. The more wood he cut away from it, the longer that bad-mannered nose grew.

After a while, he began carving a mouth.

Before he'd even finished it, though, the mouth began laughing and sneering.

"Stop being silly!" Geppetto shouted. He was furious by now, but he might as well have been shouting at the wall.

"I repeat! Stop being silly!" he roared in his most threatening voice.

The mouth stopped laughing and sneering. But now it stuck out its tongue as far as it could.

Geppetto was afraid he'd spoil his work if he paid any more attention to all this nonsense. So he pretended not to notice and went on with his carving.

He finished the mouth, and then made the puppet's chin, neck, shoulders, belly, arms, and hands.

As soon as the hands were done, he felt his wig being snatched off! He looked down, and what do you think he saw? It was his yellow wig in the puppet's brand-new hands.

"Pinocchio! Give that wig back to me!"

Instead of giving it back, Pinocchio stuck it on his own head. It almost smothered him, for it was so big it came down over his whole face.

The puppet's wildness made Geppetto terribly sad, sadder than he'd ever been before.

"You naughty little wretch!" he said. "I haven't even finished carving you and here you are, treating me, your own father, without any respect at all. Oh, that's bad, my boy, very bad!"

And he wiped away a tear from his eye.

He still hadn't made Pinocchio's legs and feet, and so he kept on carving.

No sooner had he finished the feet than one of them kicked him, right on the tip of his nose.

"It's my own fault," Geppetto said to himself. "I should have known what to expect. Well, well, it's too late now."

He picked the puppet up by the arms and set him down on the floor, to teach him to walk.

Pinocchio's legs were stiff and straight, and he didn't know how to use them. Geppetto held him by the hand and showed him how to move: first one foot, then the other.

Soon Pinocchio felt more comfortable walking. His legs relaxed, and he could take steps by himself. Then he began jumping all around the room. At last he shot out the door and sped down the street. He was running away from home!

Poor Geppetto chased after him, but couldn't catch him. Pinocchio was leaping and hopping like a wild hare. His little wooden feet clattered along the sidewalk, making as much noise as twenty men in heavy boots. He ran faster and faster.

"Grab him! Catch him!" shouted Geppetto. But the people on the street were terribly excited to see the wooden puppet tearing down the street like a racehorse. They watched in delight and laughed and laughed, and kept laughing and laughing. I can't tell you how happy the sight made them.

At last, luckily, a policeman arrived. He had heard all the clatter and shouting, and at first he thought someone's pony must have broken away from its master. He planted himself solidly in the middle of the street, with his legs wide apart, so that he could stop the runaway pony and quiet things down again.

Pinocchio saw the policeman blocking his way and decided to fool him by running right between his legs. That was a big mistake!

Deftly, without budging an inch, the policeman caught him by the nose. It was such a big, ridiculous nose that it seemed just made to be grabbed by policemen. He handed the puppet over to Geppetto, who had made up his mind to punish the little pest by boxing his ears. Imagine how embarrassed he was when he couldn't find Pinocchio's ears! Do you know why he couldn't? Because he'd been in such a hurry to finish making the puppet that he'd forgotten to carve them.

So now Geppetto took Pinocchio by the scruff of his neck and forced him to walk alongside him. Geppetto nodded fiercely and said, "At last we're going back home. When we get there, you can bet I'll make you pay for what you've done!"

At this Pinocchio flung himself to the ground and refused to go any further. All this time, of course, little groups of people with nothing better to do were gathering around and watching.

Some had one opinion. Some had another.

"Poor little puppet!" said some. "Who can blame him for not wanting to go home? Who knows what cruel things that awful Geppetto would do to him?"

Others had even worse things to say:

"Geppetto is supposed to be so nice. But he's very mean to children! If we let him keep that poor puppet, he'll probably chop him up into tiny pieces."

All in all, there was such a great fuss that the policeman set Pinocchio free and took poor old Geppetto off to jail. Geppetto couldn't think of the right words to defend himself. He could only moan like a calf. As he was led off to prison, he stammered and sobbed, "Wretched boy! And to think how hard I've tried to make him a nice young puppet! Well, it's all my fault. I should have known what to expect."

You wouldn't believe the things that happened afterwards. I'll tell you all about them soon.

Three Strong Women

Claus Stamm

Long ago, in Japan, there lived a famous wrestler, and he was on his way to the capital city to wrestle before the Emperor.

He strode down the road on legs thick as the trunks of small trees. He had been walking for seven hours and could, and probably would, walk for seven more without getting tired.

The time was autumn, the sky was a cold, watery blue, the air chilly. In the small bright sun, the trees along the roadside glowed red and orange.

The wrestler hummed to himself, "Zun-zun-zun," in time with the long swing of his legs. Wind blew through his thin brown robe, and he wore no sword at his side. He felt proud that he needed no sword, even in the darkest and loneliest places. The icy air on his body only reminded him that few tailors would have been able to

make expensive warm clothes for a man so broad and tall. He felt much as a wrestler should: strong, healthy, and rather conceited.

A soft roar of fast-moving water beyond the trees told him that he was passing above a river bank. He "zun-zunned" louder; he loved the sound of his voice and wanted it to sound clearly above the rushing water.

He thought: They call me Forever-Mountain because I am such a good strong wrestler—big, too. I'm a fine, brave man and far too modest ever to say so. . . .

Just then he saw a girl who must have come up from the river, for she steadied a bucket on her head.

Her hands on the bucket were small, and there was a dimple on each thumb, just below the knuckle. She was a round little girl with red cheeks and a nose like a

friendly button. Her eyes looked as though she were thinking of ten thousand funny stories at once. She clambered up onto the road and walked ahead of the wrestler, jolly and bounceful.

"If I don't tickle that fat girl, I shall regret it all my life," said the wrestler under his breath. "She's sure to go 'squeak' and I shall laugh and laugh. If she drops her bucket, that will be even funnier— and I can always run and fill it again and even carry it home for her."

He tiptoed up and poked her lightly in the ribs with one huge finger.

"Kochokochokocho!" he said, a fine, ticklish sound in Japanese.

The girl gave a satisfying squeal, giggled, and brought one arm down so that the wrestler's hand was caught between it and her body.

"Ho-ho-ho! You've caught me! I can't move at all!" said the wrestler, laughing.

"I know," said the jolly girl.

He felt that it was very good-tempered of her to take a joke so well, and started to pull his hand free.

Somehow, he could not.

He tried again, using a little more strength.

"Now, now—let me go, little girl," he said. "I am a very powerful man. If I pull too hard I might hurt you."

"Pull," said the girl. "I admire powerful men."

She began to walk, and though the wrestler tugged and pulled until his feet dug great furrows in the ground, he had to follow. She couldn't have paid him less attention if he had been a puppy— a small one.

Ten minutes later, still tugging while trudging helplessly after her, he was glad that the road was lonely and no one was there to see.

"Please let me go," he pleaded. "I am the famous wrestler Forever-Mountain. I must go and show my strength before the Emperor"—he burst out weeping from shame and confusion—"and you're hurting my hand!"

The girl steadied the bucket on her head with her free hand and dimpled sympathetically over her shoulder.

"You poor, sweet little Forever-Mountain," she said. "Are you tired? Shall I carry you? I can leave the water here and come back for it later."

"I do not want you to carry me. I want you to let me go, and then I want to forget I ever saw you. What do you want with me?" moaned the pitiful wrestler.

"I only want to help you," said the girl, now pulling him steadily up and up a narrow mountain path. "Oh, I am sure you'll have no more trouble than anyone else when you come up against the other wrestlers. You'll win, or else you'll lose, and you won't be too badly hurt either way. But aren't you afraid you might meet a really *strong* man someday?"

Forever-Mountain turned white. He stumbled. He was imagining being laughed at throughout Japan as "Hardly-Ever-Mountain."

She glanced back.

"You see? Tired already," she said. "I'll walk more slowly. Why

don't you come along to my mother's house and let us make a strong man of you? The wrestling in the capital isn't due to begin for three months. I know, because Grandmother thought she'd go. You'd be spending all that time in bad company and wasting what little power you have."

"All right. Three months. I'll come along," said the wrestler. He felt he had nothing more to lose. Also, he feared that the girl might become angry if he refused, and place him in the top of a tree until he changed his mind.

"Fine," she said happily. "We are almost there."

She freed his hand. It had become red and a little swollen. "But if you break your promise and run off, I shall have to chase you and carry you back."

Soon they arrived in a small valley. A simple farmhouse with a thatched roof stood in the middle.

"Grandmother is at home, but she is an old lady and she's probably sleeping." The girl shaded her eyes with one hand. "But Mother should be bringing our cow back from the field—oh, there's Mother now!"

She waved. The woman coming around the corner of the house put down the cow she was carrying and waved back.

She smiled and came across the grass, walking with a lively bounce like her daughter. "These mountain paths are full of stones. They hurt the cow's feet. And who is the nice young man you've brought, Maru-me?"

The girl explained. "And we have only three months!" she finished anxiously.

"Well, it's not long enough to do much, but it's not so short a time that we can't do something," said her mother, looking thoughtful. "But he does look terribly feeble. He'll need a lot of good things to eat. Maybe when he gets stronger he can help Grandmother with some of the easy work about the house."

"That will be fine!" said the girl, and she called her grandmother—loudly, for the old lady was a little deaf.

"I'm coming!" came a creaky voice from inside the house, and a little old woman leaning on a stick and looking very sleepy tottered out of the door. As she came toward them she stumbled over the roots of a great oak tree.

"Heh! My eyes aren't what they used to be. That's the fourth time this month I've stumbled over that tree," she complained and, wrapping her skinny arms about its trunk, pulled it out of the ground.

"Oh, Grandmother! You should have let me pull it up for you," said Maru-me.

"Hm. I hope I didn't hurt my poor old back," muttered the old lady. She called out. "Daughter! Throw that tree away like a good girl, so no one will fall over it. But make sure it doesn't hit anybody."

"You can help Mother with the tree," Maru-me said to Forever-Mountain. "On second thought, you'd better not help. Just watch."

Her mother went to the tree, picked it up in her two hands, and threw it—clumsily and with a little gasp. . . . Up went the tree, sailing end over end, growing smaller and smaller as it flew. It landed with a faint crash far up the mountainside.

"Ah, how clumsy," she said. "I meant to throw it *over* the mountain. It's probably blocking the path now, and I'll have to get up early tomorrow to move it."

The wrestler was not listening. He had very quietly fainted.

"Oh! We must put him to bed," said Maru-me.

"Poor, feeble young man," said her mother.

"I hope we can do something for him. Here, let me carry him, he's light," said the grandmother. She slung him over her shoulder and carried him into the house, creaking along with her cane.

The next day they began the work of making Forever-Mountain over into what they thought a strong man should be. They gave him the simplest food to eat, and the toughest. Day by day they prepared his rice with less and less water, until no ordinary man could have chewed or digested it.

Every day he was made to do the work of five men, and every

196

evening he wrestled with Grandmother. Maru-me and her mother agreed that Grandmother, being old and feeble, was the least likely to injure him accidentally. They hoped the exercise might be good for the old lady's rheumatism.

He grew stronger and stronger but was hardly aware of it. Grandmother could still throw him easily into the air—and catch him again—without ever changing her sweet old smile.

He quite forgot that outside this valley he was one of the greatest wrestlers in Japan and was called Forever-Mountain. His legs had been like logs; now they were like pillars. His big hands were hard as stones, and when he cracked his knuckles the sound was like trees splitting on a cold night.

Sometimes he did an exercise that wrestlers do in Japan—raising one foot high above the ground and bringing it down with a crash. Then people in nearby villages looked up at the winter sky and told one another that it was very late in the year for thunder.

Soon he could pull up a tree as well as the grandmother. He could even throw one—but only a small distance. One evening, near the end of his third month, he wrestled with Grandmother and held her down for half a minute.

"Heh-heh!" She chortled and got up, smiling with every wrinkle. "I would never have believed it!"

Maru-me squealed with joy and threw her arms around him—gently, for she was afraid of cracking his ribs.

"Very good, very good! What a strong man," said her mother, who had just come home from the fields, carrying, as usual, the cow. She put the cow down and patted the wrestler on the back.

They agreed that he was now ready to show some *real* strength before the Emperor.

"Take the cow along with you tomorrow when you go," said the mother. "Sell her and buy yourself a belt—a silken belt. Buy the fattest and heaviest one you can find. Wear it when you appear before the Emperor, as a souvenir from us."

"I wouldn't think of taking your only cow. You've already done too much for me. And you'll need her to plow the field, won't you?"

They burst out laughing, Maru-me squealed, her mother roared. The grandmother cackled so hard and long that she choked and had to be pounded on the back.

"Oh, dear," said the mother, still laughing. "You didn't think we used our cow for anything like *work*! Why, Grandmother here is stronger than five cows!"

"The cow is our pet," Maru-me giggled. "She has lovely brown eyes."

"But it really gets tiresome having to carry her back and forth each day so that she has enough grass to eat," said her mother.

"Then you must let me give you all the prize money that I win," said Forever-Mountain.

"Oh, no! We wouldn't think of it!" said Maru-me. "Because we all like you too much to sell you anything. And it is not proper to accept gifts of money from strangers."

"True," said Forever-Mountain. "I will now ask your mother's and grandmother's permission to marry you. I want to be one of the family."

"Oh! I'll get a wedding dress ready!" said Maru-me.

The mother and grandmother pretended to consider very seriously, but they quickly agreed.

Next morning Forever-Mountain tied his hair up in the topknot that all Japanese wrestlers wear, and got ready to leave. He thanked Maru-me and her mother and bowed very low to the grandmother, since she was the oldest and had been a fine wrestling partner.

Then he picked up the cow in his arms and trudged up the mountain. When he reached the top, he slung the cow over one shoulder and waved good-bye to Maru-me.

At the first town he came to, Forever-Mountain sold the cow. She brought a good price because she was unusually fat from never having worked in her life. With the money, he bought the heaviest silken belt he could find.

When he reached the palace grounds, many of the other wrestlers were already there, sitting about, eating enormous bowls of rice, comparing one another's weight, and telling stories. They

paid little attention to Forever-Mountain, except to wonder why he had arrived so late this year. Some of them noticed that he had grown quiet and took no part at all in their boasting.

All the ladies and gentlemen of the court were waiting in a special courtyard for the wrestling to begin. They wore many robes, one on top of another, heavy with embroidery and gold cloth, and sweat ran down their faces and froze in the winter afternoon. The gentlemen had long swords so weighted with gold and precious stones that they could never have used them, even if they had known how. The court ladies, with their long black hair hanging down behind, had their faces painted dead white, which made them look frightened. They had pulled out their real eyebrows and painted new ones high above the place where eyebrows are supposed to be, and this made them all look as though they were very surprised at something.

Behind a screen sat the Emperor—by himself, because he was too noble for ordinary people to look at. He was a lonely old man with a kind, tired face. He hoped the wrestling would end quickly so that he could go to his room and write poems.

The first two wrestlers chosen to fight were Forever-Mountain and a wrestler who was said to have the biggest stomach in the country. He and Forever-Mountain both threw some salt into the ring. It was understood that this drove away evil spirits.

Then the other wrestler, moving his stomach somewhat out of the way, raised his foot and brought it down with a fearful stamp. He glared at Forever-Mountain as if to say, "Now *you* stamp, you poor frightened man!"

Forever-Mountain raised his foot. He brought it down.

There was a sound like thunder, the earth shook, and the other wrestler bounced into the air and out of the ring, as gracefully as any soap bubble.

He picked himself up and bowed to the Emperor's screen.

"The earth-god is angry. Possibly there is something the matter with the salt," he said. "I do not think I shall wrestle this season." And he walked out, looking very suspiciously over one shoulder at Forever-Mountain.

From then on, Forever-Mountain brought his foot down lightly. As each wrestler came into the ring, he picked him up very gently, carried him out, and placed him before the Emperor's screen, bowing most courteously every time.

The court ladies' eyebrows went up even higher. The gentlemen looked disturbed and a little afraid. They loved to see fierce, strong men tugging and grunting at each other, but Forever-Mountain was a little too much for them. Only the Emperor was happy behind his screen, for now, with the wrestling over so quickly, he would have that much more time to write his poems. He ordered all the prize money handed over to Forever-Mountain.

"But," he said, "you had better not wrestle any more." He stuck a finger through his screen and waggled it at the other wrestlers, who were sitting on the ground weeping with disappointment like great fat babies.

Forever-Mountain promised not to wrestle any more. Everybody looked relieved. The wrestlers sitting on the ground almost smiled.

"I think I shall become a farmer," Forever-Mountain said,

and left at once to go back to Maru-me.

Maru-me was waiting for him. When she saw him coming, she ran down the mountain, picked him up, together with the heavy bags of prize money, and carried him halfway up the mountainside. Then she giggled and put him down. The rest of the way she let him carry her.

Forever-Mountain kept his promise to the Emperor and never fought in public again. His name was forgotten in the capital. But up in the mountains, sometimes, the earth shakes and rumbles, and they say that is Forever-Mountain and Maru-me's grandmother practicing wrestling in the hidden valley.

Nature and wisdom always say the same.

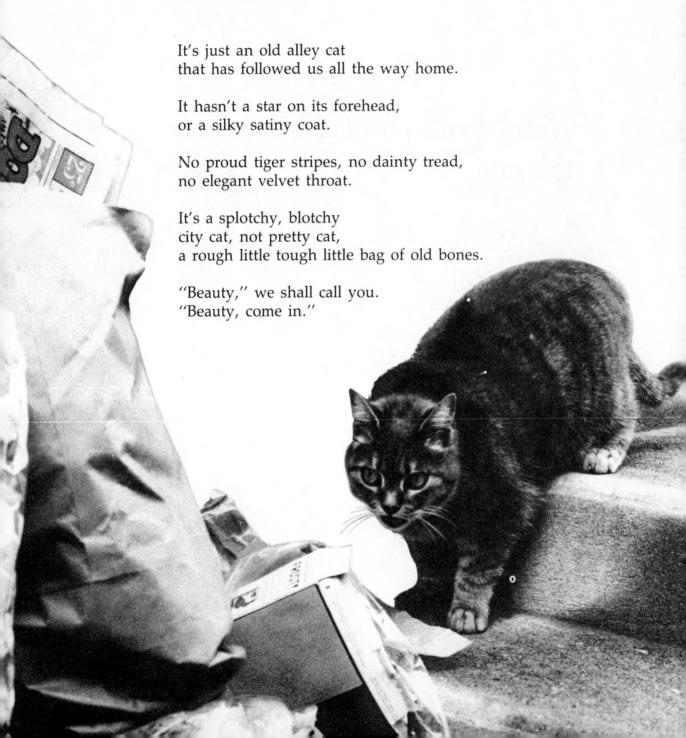

The Stray Cat

Eve Merriam

It's just an old alley cat
that has followed us all the way home.

It hasn't a star on its forehead,
or a silky satiny coat.

No proud tiger stripes, no dainty tread,
no elegant velvet throat.

It's a splotchy, blotchy
city cat, not pretty cat,
a rough little tough little bag of old bones.

"Beauty," we shall call you.
"Beauty, come in."

Zlateh the Goat

Isaac Bashevis Singer

At Hanukkah time, the road from the village to the town is usually covered with snow, but this year the winter had been a mild one. Hanukkah had almost come, yet little snow had fallen. The sun shone most of the time. The peasants complained that because of the dry weather there would be a poor harvest of winter grain. New grass sprouted, and the peasants sent their cattle out to pasture.

For Reuven, the furrier, it was a bad year, and after long hesitation he decided to sell Zlateh the goat. She was old and gave little milk.

Feyvel, the town butcher, had offered eight gulden for her. Such a sum would buy Hanukkah candles, potatoes and oil for pancakes, gifts for the children, and other holiday necessaries for the house. Reuven told his oldest boy Aaron to take the goat to town.

Aaron understood what taking the goat to Feyvel meant, but he had to obey his father. Leah, his mother, wiped the tears from her eyes when she heard the news. Aaron's younger sisters, Anna and Miriam, cried loudly. Aaron put on his quilted jacket and a cap with earmuffs, bound a rope around Zlateh's neck, and took along two slices of bread with cheese to eat on the road. Aaron was supposed to deliver the goat by evening, spend the night at the butcher's, and return the next day with the money.

While the family said goodbye to the goat, and Aaron placed the rope around her neck, Zlateh stood as patiently and good-naturedly as ever. She licked Reuven's hand. She shook her small white beard. Zlateh trusted human beings. She knew that they always fed her and never did her any harm.

When Aaron brought her out on the road to town, she seemed somewhat astonished. She'd never been led in that direction before. She looked back at him questioningly, as if to say, "Where are you taking me?" But after a while she seemed to come to the conclusion that a goat shouldn't ask questions. Still, the road was different. They passed new fields, pastures, and huts with thatched roofs. Here and there a dog barked and came running after them, but Aaron chased it away with his stick.

The sun was shining when Aaron left the village. Suddenly the weather changed. A large black cloud with a bluish center appeared in the east and spread itself rapidly over the sky. A cold wind blew in with it. The crows flew low, croaking. At first it looked as if it would rain, but instead it began to hail as in summer. It was early in the day, but it became dark as dusk. After a while, the hail turned to snow.

In his twelve years, Aaron had seen all kinds of weather, but he had never experienced a snow like this one. It was so dense it shut out the light of the day. In a short time their path was completely covered. The wind became as cold as ice. The road to town was narrow and winding. Aaron no longer knew where he was. He could not see through the snow. The cold soon penetrated his quilted jacket.

At first Zlateh didn't seem to mind the change in weather. She too was twelve years old and knew what winter meant. But when her legs sank deeper and deeper into the snow, she began to turn her head and look at Aaron in wonderment. Her mild eyes seemed to ask, "Why are we out in such a storm?" Aaron hoped that a peasant would come along with his cart, but no one passed by.

The snow grew thicker, falling to the ground in large, whirling flakes. Beneath it Aaron's boots touched the softness of a plowed field. He realized that he was no longer on the road. He had gone astray. He could no longer figure out which was east or west, which way was the village, the town. The wind whistled, howled, whirled the snow about in eddies. It looked as if white imps were playing tag on

the fields. A white dust rose above the ground. Zlateh stopped. She could walk no longer. Stubbornly she anchored her cleft hooves in the earth and bleated as if pleading to be taken home. Icicles hung from her white beard, and her horns were glazed with frost.

Aaron did not want to admit the danger, but he knew just the same that if they did not find shelter, they would freeze to death. This was no ordinary storm. It was a mighty blizzard. The snowfall had reached his knees. His hands were numb, and he could no longer feel his toes. He choked when he breathed. His nose felt like wood, and he rubbed it with snow. Zlateh's bleating began to sound like crying. Those humans in whom

she had so much confidence had dragged her into a trap. Aaron began to pray to God for himself and for the innocent animal.

Suddenly he made out the shape of a hill. He wondered what it could be. Who had piled snow into such a huge heap? He moved toward it, dragging Zlateh after him. When he came near it, he realized that it was a large haystack which the snow had blanketed.

Aaron realized immediately that they were saved. With great effort he dug his way through the snow. He was a village boy and knew what to do. When he reached the hay, he hollowed out a nest for himself and the goat. No matter how cold it may be outside, in the hay it is always warm. And hay was food for Zlateh. The moment she smelled it, she became contented and began to eat. Outside the snow continued to fall. It quickly covered the passageway Aaron had dug. But a boy and an animal need to breathe, and there was hardly any air in their hideout. Aaron bored a kind of a window through the hay and snow and carefully kept the passage clear.

Zlateh, having eaten her fill, sat down on her hind legs and seemed to have regained her confidence in man. Aaron ate his two slices of bread and cheese, but after the difficult journey he was still hungry. He looked at Zlateh and noticed her udders were full. He lay down next to her, placing himself so that when he milked her, he could squirt the milk into his mouth. It was rich and sweet. Zlateh was not accustomed to being milked that way, but she did not resist. On the contrary, she seemed eager to reward Aaron for bringing her to a shelter whose very walls, floor, and ceiling were made of food.

Through the window Aaron could catch a glimpse of the chaos outside. The wind carried before it whole drifts of snow. It was completely dark, and he did not know whether night had already come or whether it was the darkness of the storm. Thank God that in the hay it was not cold. The dried hay, grass, and field flowers exuded the warmth of the summer sun. Zlateh ate frequently; she nibbled from above, below, from the left and right. Her body gave forth an animal warmth, and Aaron cuddled up to her. He had always loved Zlateh, but now she was like a sister. He was alone, cut off from his family, and wanted to talk. He began to talk to Zlateh.

"Zlateh, what do you think about what has happened to us?" he asked.

"Maaaa," Zlateh answered.

"If we hadn't found this stack of hay, we would both be frozen stiff by now," Aaron said.

"Maaaa," was the goat's reply.

"If the snow keeps falling like this, we may have to stay here for days," Aaron explained.

"Maaaa," Zlateh bleated.

"What does 'Maaaa' mean?" Aaron asked. "You'd better speak up clearly."

"Maaaa. Maaaa," Zlateh tried.

"Well, let it be 'Maaaa' then," Aaron said patiently. "You can't speak, but I know you understand. I need you and you need me. Isn't that right?"

"Maaaa."

Aaron became sleepy. He made a pillow out of some hay, leaned his head on it, and dozed off. Zlateh too fell asleep.

When Aaron opened his eyes, he didn't know whether it was morning or night. The snow had blocked up his window. He tried to clear it, but when he had bored through to the length of his arm, he still hadn't reached the outside. Luckily he had his stick with him and was able to break through to the open air. It was still dark outside. The snow continued to fall and the wind wailed, first with one voice and then with many. Sometimes it had the sound of devilish laughter. Zlateh too awoke, and when Aaron greeted her, she answered, "Maaaa." Yes, Zlateh's language consisted of only one word, but it meant many things. Now she was saying, "We must accept all that God gives us—heat, cold, hunger, satisfaction, light, and darkness."

Aaron had awakened hungry. He had eaten up his food, but Zlateh had plenty of milk.

For three days Aaron and Zlateh stayed in the haystack.

Aaron had always loved Zlateh, but in these three days he loved her more and more. She fed him with her milk and helped him keep warm. She comforted him with her patience. He told her many stories, and she always cocked her ears and listened. When he patted her, she licked his hand and his face. Then she said, "Maaaa," and he knew it meant, I love you too.

The snow fell for three days, though after the first day it was not as thick, and the wind quieted down. Sometimes Aaron felt that there could never have been a summer, that the snow had always fallen, ever since he could remember. He, Aaron, never had a father or mother or sisters. He was a snow child, born of the snow, and so was Zlateh. It was so quiet in the hay that his ears rang in the stillness. Aaron and Zlateh slept all night and a good part of the day. As for Aaron's dreams, they were all about warm weather. He dreamed of green fields, trees covered with blossoms, clear brooks, and singing birds. By the third night the snow had stopped, but Aaron did not dare to find his way home in the darkness. The sky became clear, and the moon shone, casting silvery nets on the snow. Aaron dug his way out and looked at the world. It was all white, quiet, dreaming dreams of heavenly splendor. The stars were large and close. The moon swam in the sky as in a sea.

On the morning of the fourth day Aaron heard the ringing of sleigh bells. The haystack was not far from the road. The peasant who drove the sleigh pointed out the way to him—not to the town and Feyvel, the butcher, but home to the village. Aaron had decided in the haystack that he would never part with Zlateh.

Aaron's family and their neighbors had searched for the boy and the goat but had found no trace of them during the storm. They feared they were lost. Aaron's mother and sisters cried for him; his father remained silent and gloomy. Suddenly one of the neighbors came running to their house with the news that Aaron and Zlateh were coming up the road.

There was great joy in the family. Aaron told them how he had found the stack of hay and how Zlateh had fed him with her milk. Aaron's sisters kissed and hugged Zlateh and gave her a special treat of chopped carrots and potato peels, which Zlateh gobbled up hungrily.

Nobody ever again thought of selling Zlateh, and now that the cold weather had finally set in, the villagers needed the services of Reuven, the furrier, once more. When Hanukkah came, Aaron's mother was able to fry pancakes every evening, and Zlateh got her portion too. Even though Zlateh had her own pen, she often came to the kitchen, knocking on the door with her horns to indicate that she was ready to visit; and she was always admitted. In the evening Aaron, Miriam, and Anna played dreidel. Zlateh sat near the stove watching the children and the flickering of the Hanukkah candles.

Once in a while Aaron would ask her, "Zlateh, do you remember the three days we spent together?"

And Zlateh would scratch her neck with a horn, shake her white bearded head, and come out with the single sound which expressed all her thoughts, and all her love.

The Tiger Behind the Fox

Chan Kuo Ts′e

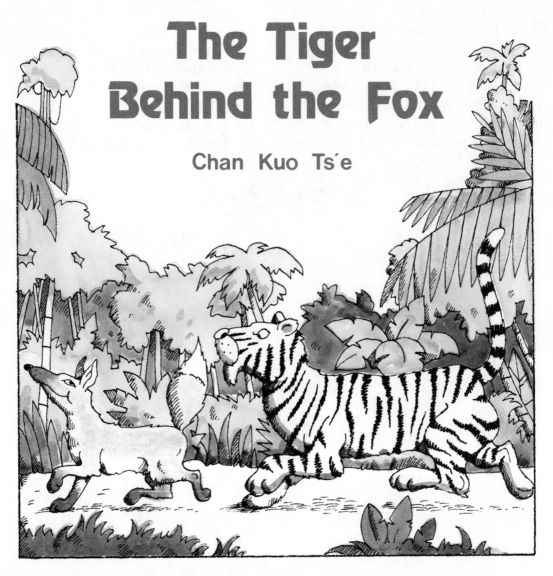

A tiger caught a fox. The fox said, "You wouldn't dare eat *me!* The gods in Heaven have made me the leader of all animals. It would be a violation of the gods' mandate for you to make a meal of me. If you doubt it, let me walk in front, and you follow to see if any animal dares stand his ground." The tiger consented and went with the fox, nose to heels. Every animal that saw them fled. Amazed, and agreeing that the fox was leader of all the animals, the tiger went on his way.

excerpt from
Bambi
A Life in the Woods

Felix Salten

He came into the world in the middle of the thicket, in one of those little, hidden forest glades which seem to be entirely open but are really screened in on all sides. There was very little room in it, scarcely enough for him and his mother.

He stood there, swaying unsteadily on his thin legs and staring vaguely in front of him with clouded eyes which saw nothing. He hung his head, trembled a great deal, and was still completely stunned.

"What a beautiful child," cried the magpie.

She had flown past, attracted by the deep groans the mother uttered in her labor. The magpie perched on a neighboring branch. "What a beautiful child," she kept repeating. Receiving no answer, she went on talkatively, "How amazing to think that he should be able to get right up and walk! How interesting! I've never seen the like of it before in all my born days. Of course, I'm still young, only a year out of the nest you might say. But I think it's wonderful. A child like that, hardly a minute in this world, and beginning to walk already! I call that remarkable. Really, I find that everything you deer do is remarkable. Can he run too?"

"Of course," replied the mother softly. "But you must pardon me if I don't talk with you now. I have so much to do, and I still feel a little faint."

"Don't put yourself out on my account," said the
magpie. "I have very little time myself. But you don't see a
sight like this every day. Think what a care and bother
such things mean to us. The children can't stir once they
are out of the egg but lie helpless in the nest and require
an attention, an attention, I repeat, of which you simply
can't have any comprehension. What a labor it is to feed
them, what a trouble to watch them. Just think for a
moment what a strain it is to hunt food for the children
and to have to be eternally on guard lest something
happen to them. They are helpless if you are not with
them. Isn't it the truth? And how long it is before they can
move, how long it is before they get their feathers and
look like anything at all."

"Pardon," replied the mother, "I wasn't listening."

The magpie flew off. "A stupid soul," she thought to
herself, "very nice, but stupid."

The mother scarcely noticed that she was gone. She
continued zealously washing her newly-born. She washed
him with her tongue, fondling and caressing his body in a
sort of warm massage.

The slight thing staggered a little. Under the strokes of
her tongue, which softly touched him here and there, he
drew himself together and stood still. His little red coat,
that was still somewhat tousled, bore fine white spots, and

on his vague baby face there was still a deep, sleepy expression.

Round about grew hazel bushes, dogwoods, blackthorns and young elders. Tall maples, beeches and oaks wove a green roof over the thicket and from the firm, dark-brown earth sprang fern fronds, wood vetch and sage. Underneath, the leaves of the violets, which had already bloomed, and of the strawberries, which were just beginning, clung to the ground. Through the thick foliage, the early sunlight filtered in a golden web. The whole forest resounded with myriad voices, was penetrated by them in a joyous agitation. The wood thrush rejoiced incessantly, the doves cooed without stopping, the blackbirds whistled, finches warbled, the titmice chirped. Through the midst of these songs the jay flew, uttering its quarrelsome cry, the magpie mocked them, and the pheasants cackled loud and high. At times the shrill exulting of a woodpecker rose above all the other voices. The call of the falcon shrilled, light and piercing, over the treetops, and the hoarse crow chorus was heard continuously.

The little fawn understood not one of the many songs and calls, not a word of the conversations. He did not even listen to them. Nor did he heed any of the odors which blew through the woods. He heard only the soft licking against his coat that washed him and warmed him and kissed him. And he smelled nothing but his mother's body near him. She smelled good to him and, snuggling closer to her, he hunted eagerly around and found nourishment for his life.

While he suckled, the mother continued to caress her little one. "Bambi," she whispered. Every little while she raised her head and, listening, snuffed the wind. Then she kissed her fawn again, reassured and happy.

"Bambi," she repeated. "My little Bambi."

In early summer the trees stood still under the blue sky, held their limbs outstretched and received the direct rays of the sun. On the shrubs and bushes in the undergrowth, the flowers unfolded their red, white and yellow stars. On some the seed pods had begun to appear again. They perched innumerable on the fine tips of the branches, tender and firm and resolute, and seemed like small, clenched fists. Out of the earth came whole troops of flowers, like motley stars, so that the soil of the twilit forest floor shone with a silent, ardent, colorful gladness. Everything smelled of fresh leaves, of blossoms, of moist clods and green wood. When morning broke, or when the sun went down, the whole woods resounded with a thousand voices, and from morning til night, the bees hummed, the wasps droned, and filled the fragrant stillness with their murmur.

These were the earliest days of Bambi's life. He walked behind his mother on a narrow track that ran through the midst of the bushes. How pleasant it was to walk there. The thick foliage stroked his flanks softly and bent supplely aside. The track appeared to be barred and obstructed in a dozen places, and yet they advanced with the greatest ease. There were tracks like this everywhere, running crisscross through the whole woods. His mother knew them all, and if Bambi sometimes stopped before a bush as if it were an impenetrable green wall, she always found where the path went through, without hesitation or searching.

Bambi questioned her. He loved to ask his mother questions. It was the pleasantest thing for him to ask a question and then to hear what answer his mother would give. Bambi was never surprised that question after question should come into his mind continually and without effort. He found it perfectly natural, and it delighted him very much. It was very delightful, too, to wait expectantly till the answer came. If it turned out the way he wanted, he was satisfied. Sometimes, of course, he did not understand, but that was pleasant also because he was kept busy picturing what he had not understood, in his own way. Sometimes he felt very sure that his mother was not giving him a complete answer, was intentionally not telling him all she knew. And at first, that was very pleasant, too. For then there would remain in him such a lively curiosity, such suspicion, mysteriously and joyously flashing through him, such anticipation, that he would become anxious and happy at the same time, and grow silent.

Once he asked, "Whom does this trail belong to, Mother?"

His mother answered, "To us."

Bambi asked again, "To you and me?"

"Yes."

"To us two?"

"Yes."

"Only to us two?"

"No," said his mother, "to us deer."

"What are deer?" Bambi asked, and laughed.

His mother looked at him from head to foot and laughed too. "You are a deer and I am a deer. We're both deer," she said. "Do you understand?"

Bambi sprang into the air for joy. "Yes, I understand," he said. "I'm a little deer and you're a big deer, aren't you?"

His mother nodded and said, "Now you see."

But Bambi grew serious again. "Are there other deer besides you and me?" he asked.

"Certainly," his mother said. "Many of them."

"Where are they?" cried Bambi.

"Here, everywhere."

"But I don't see them."

"You will soon," she said.

"When?" Bambi stood still, wild with curiosity.

"Soon." The mother walked on quietly. Bambi followed her. He kept silent for he was wondering what "soon" might mean. He came to the conclusion that "soon" was certainly not "now." But he wasn't sure at what time "soon" stopped being "soon" and began to be "a long while." Suddenly he asked, "Who made this trail?"

"We," his mother answered.

Bambi was astonished. "We? You and I?"

The mother said, "Well, we . . . we deer."

Bambi asked, "Which deer?"

"All of us," his mother said sharply.

They walked on. Bambi was in high spirits and felt like leaping off the path, but he stayed close to his mother. Something rustled in front of them, close to the ground. The fern fronds and wood lettuce concealed something that advanced in violent motion. A threadlike little cry shrilled

out piteously; then all was still. Only the leaves and the blades of grass shivered back into place. A ferret had caught a mouse. He came slinking by, slid sideways, and prepared to enjoy his meal.

"What was that?" asked Bambi excitedly.

"Nothing," his mother soothed him.

"But," Bambi trembled, "but I saw it."

"Yes, yes," said his mother. "Don't be frightened. The ferret has killed a mouse." But Bambi was dreadfully frightened. A vast, unknown horror clutched at his heart. It was long before he could speak again. Then he asked, "Why did he kill the mouse?"

"Because—" his mother hesitated. "Let us walk faster," she said, as though something had just occurred to her and as though she had forgotten the question. She began to hurry. Bambi sprang after her.

A long pause ensued. They walked on quietly again. Finally Bambi asked anxiously, "Shall we kill a mouse, too, sometime?"

"No," replied his mother.

"Never?" asked Bambi.

"Never," came the answer.

"Why not?" asked Bambi, relieved.

"Because we never kill anything," said his mother simply.

Bambi grew happy again.

Loud cries were coming from a young ash tree which stood near their path. The mother went along without noticing them, but Bambi stopped inquisitively. Overhead two jays were quarreling about a nest they had plundered.

"Get away, you murderer!" cried one.

"Keep cool, you fool," the other answered, "I'm not afraid of you."

"Look for your own nests," the first one shouted, "or I'll break your head for you." He was beside himself with rage. "What vulgarity!" he chattered. "What vulgarity!"

The other jay had spied Bambi and fluttered down a few branches to shout at him. "What are you gawking at, you freak?" he screamed.

Bambi sprang away, terrified. He reached his mother and walked behind her again, frightened and obedient, thinking she had not noticed his absence.

After a pause he asked, "Mother, what is vulgarity?"

"I don't know," said his mother.

Bambi thought a while; then he began again. "Why were they both so angry with each other, Mother?" he asked.

"They were fighting over food," his mother answered.

"Will we fight over food, too, sometime?" Bambi asked.

"No," said his mother.

Bambi asked, "Why not?"

"Because there is enough for all of us," his mother replied.

Bambi wanted to know something else. "Mother," he began.

"What is it?"

"Will we be angry with each other sometime?" he asked.

"No, child," said his mother, "we don't do such things."

They walked along again. Presently it grew light ahead of them. It grew very bright. The trail ended with the tangle of vines and bushes. A few steps more and they would be in the bright open space that spread out before them. Bambi wanted to bound forward, but his mother had stopped.

"What is it?" he asked impatiently, already delighted.

"It's the meadow," his mother answered.

"What is a meadow?" asked Bambi insistently.

His mother cut him short. "You'll soon find out for yourself," she said. She had become very serious and watchful. She stood motionless, holding her head high and listening intently. She sucked in deep breathfuls of air and looked very severe.

"It's all right," she said at last, "we can go out."

Bambi leaped forward, but his mother barred the way.

"Wait till I call you," she said. Bambi obeyed at once and stood still. "That's right," said his mother, to encourage him, "and now listen to what I am saying to you." Bambi heard how seriously his mother spoke and felt terribly excited.

"Walking on the meadow is not so simple," his mother went on. "It's a difficult and dangerous business. Don't ask me why. You'll find that out later on. Now do exactly as I tell you to. Will you?"

"Yes," Bambi promised.

"Good," said his mother. "I'm going out alone first. Stay here and wait. And don't take your eyes off me for a minute. If you see me run back here, then turn round and run as fast as you can. I'll catch up with you soon." She grew silent and seemed to be thinking. Then she went on earnestly. "Run away as fast as your legs will carry you. Run even if something should happen . . . even if you should see me fall to the ground. . . . Don't think of me, do you understand? No matter what you see or hear, start running right away and just as fast as you possibly can. Do you promise me to do that?"

"Yes," said Bambi softly. His mother spoke so seriously.

She went on speaking. "Out there if I should call you," she said, "there must be no looking around and no questions, but you must get behind me instantly. Understand that. Run without pausing or stopping to think. If I begin to run, that means for you to run, too, and no stopping until we are back here again. You won't forget, will you?"

"No," said Bambi in a troubled voice.

"Now I'm going ahead," said his mother, and seemed to become calmer.

She walked out. Bambi, who never took his eyes off her, saw how she moved forward with slow, cautious steps. He stood there full of expectancy, full of fear and curiosity. He saw how his mother listened in all directions, saw her shrink together, and shrank together himself, ready to leap back into the thickets. Then his mother grew calm again. She stretched herself. Then she looked around satisfied and called, "Come!"

Bambi bounded out. Joy seized him with such tremendous force that he forgot his worries in a flash. Through the thicket he could see only the green treetops overhead. Once in a while he caught a glimpse of the blue sky.

Now he saw the whole heaven stretching far and wide, and he rejoiced without knowing why. In the forest he had seen only a stray sunbeam now and then, or the tender, dappled light that played through the branches.

Suddenly he was standing in the blinding hot sunlight whose boundless power was beaming upon him. He stood in the splendid warmth that made him shut his eyes but which opened his heart.

Bambi was as though bewitched. He was completely beside himself with pleasure. He was simply wild. He leaped into the air three, four, five times. He had to do it. He felt a terrible desire to leap and jump. He stretched his young limbs joyfully. His breath came deeply and easily. He drank in the air. The sweet smell of the meadow made him so wildly happy that he had to leap into the air.

Bambi was a child. If he had been a human child he would have shouted. But he was a young deer, and deer cannot shout, at least not the way human children do. So he rejoiced with his legs and with his whole body as he flung himself into the air. His mother stood by and was glad. She saw that Bambi was wild. She watched how he bounded into the air and fell again awkwardly, in one spot. She saw how he stared around him, dazed and bewildered, only to leap up over and over again. She understood that Bambi knew only the narrow deer tracks in the forest and how his brief life was used to the limits of the thicket. He did not move from one place because he did not understand how to run freely around the open meadow.

So she stretched out her forefeet and bent laughingly toward Bambi for a moment. Then she was off with one bound, racing around in a circle so that the tall grass stems swished.

Bambi was frightened and stood motionless. Was that a sign for him to run back to the thicket? His mother had said to him, "Don't worry about me no matter what you see or hear. Just run as fast as you can." He was going to turn around and run as she had commanded him to, but his mother came galloping up suddenly. She came up with a wonderful swishing sound and stopped two steps from him. She bent toward him, laughing as she had at first, and cried, "Catch me." And in a flash she was gone.

Bambi was puzzled. What did she mean? Then she came back again running so fast that it made him giddy.

She pushed his flank with her nose and said quickly, "Try to catch me," and fled away.

Bambi started after her. He took a few steps. Then his steps became short bounds. He felt as if he were flying

without any effort on his part. There was a space under
his hoofs, space under his bounding feet, space and still
more space. Bambi was beside himself with joy.

The swishing grass sounded wonderful to his ears. It
was marvelously soft and as fine as silk where it brushed
against him. He ran around in a circle. He turned and flew
off in a new circle, turned around again and kept running.

His mother was standing still, getting her breath again.
She kept following Bambi with her eyes. He was wild.

Suddenly the race was over. He stopped and came up
to his mother, lifting his hoofs elegantly. He looked
joyfully at her. Then they strolled contentedly side by side.

Since he had been in the open, Bambi had felt the sky
and the sun and the green meadow with his whole body.
He took one blinding, giddy glance at the sun, and he felt
its rays as they lay warmly on his back.

Presently he began to enjoy the meadow with his eyes
also. Its wonders amazed him at every step he took. You
could not see the tiniest speck of earth the way you could
in the forest. Blade after blade of grass covered every inch
of the ground. It tossed and waved luxuriantly. It bent
softly aside under every footstep, only to rise up unharmed
again. The broad green meadow was starred with white
daisies, with the thick, round red and purple clover
blossoms and bright, golden dandelion heads.

"Look, look, Mother!" Bambi exclaimed. "There's a
flower flying."

"That's not a flower," said his mother, "that's a
butterfly."

Bambi stared at the butterfly, entranced. It had darted
lightly from a blade of grass and was fluttering about in its
giddy way. Then Bambi saw that there were many
butterflies flying in the air above the meadow. They
seemed to be in a hurry and yet moved slowly, fluttering
up and down in a sort of game that delighted him. They
really did look like gay flying flowers that would not stay
on their stems but had unfastened themselves in order to
dance a little. They looked, too, like flowers that come to
rest at sundown but have no fixed places and have to hunt
for them, dropping down and vanishing as if they really
had settled somewhere, yet always flying up again, a little

way at first, then higher and higher, and always searching
farther and farther because all the good places have already
been taken.

Bambi gazed at them all. He would have loved to see
one close by. He wanted to see one face to face but he
could not. They flew in and out continually. The air was
aflutter with them.

When he looked down at the ground again he was
delighted with the thousands of living things he saw
stirring under his hoofs. They ran and jumped in all
directions. He would see a wild swarm of them, and the
next moment they had disappeared in the grass again.

"Who are they, Mother?" he asked.

"Those are ants," his mother answered.

"Look," cried Bambi, "see that piece of grass jumping.
Look how high it can jump!"

"That's not grass," his mother explained, "that's a nice
grasshopper."

"Why does he jump that way?" asked Bambi.

"Because we're walking here," his mother answered;
"he's afraid we'll step on him."

"Oh," said Bambi, turning to the grasshopper, who
was sitting on a daisy; "oh," he said again politely, "you
don't have to be afraid; we won't hurt you."

"I'm not afraid," the grasshopper replied in a
quavering voice; "I was only frightened for a moment
when I was talking to my wife."

"Excuse us for disturbing you," said Bambi shyly.

"Not at all," the grasshopper quavered. "Since it's
you, its perfectly all right. But you never know who's
coming and you have to be careful."

"This is the first time in my life that I've ever been on
the meadow," Bambi explained; "my mother brought
me . . ."

The grasshopper was sitting with his head lowered as
though he were going to butt. He put on a serious face
and murmured, "That doesn't interest me at all. I haven't
time to stand here gossiping with you. I have to be looking
for my wife. Hopp!" And he gave a jump.

"Hopp!" said Bambi in surprise at the high jump with
which the grasshopper vanished.

Bambi ran to his mother. "Mother, I spoke to him," he cried.

"To whom?" his mother asked.

"To the grasshopper," Bambi said, "I spoke to him. He was very nice to me. And I like him so much. He's so wonderful and green and you can see through his sides. They look like leaves, but you can't see through a leaf."

"Those are his wings," said his mother.

"Oh," Bambi went on, "and his face is so serious and wise. But he was very nice to me anyhow. And how he can jump! 'Hopp!' he said, and he jumped so high I couldn't see him any more."

They walked on. The conversation with the grasshopper had excited Bambi and tired him a little, for it was the first time he had ever spoken to a stranger. He felt hungry and pressed close to his mother to be nursed.

Then he stood quietly and gazed dreamily into space for a little while with a sort of joyous ecstasy that came over him every time he was nursed by his mother. He noticed a bright flower moving in the tangled grasses. Bambi looked more closely at it. No, it wasn't a flower, but a butterfly. Bambi crept closer.

The butterfly hung heavily to a grass stem and fanned its wings slowly.

"Please sit still," Bambi said.

"Why should I sit still? I'm a butterfly," the insect answered in astonishment.

"Oh, please sit still, just for a minute," Bambi pleaded; "I've wanted so much to see you close to. Please."

"Well," said the butterfly, "for your sake I will, but not for long."

Bambi stood in front of him. "How beautiful you are!" he cried, fascinated. "How wonderfully beautiful, like a flower!"

"What?" cried the butterfly, fanning his wings. "Did you say like a flower? In my circle it's generally supposed that we're handsomer than flowers."

Bambi was embarrassed. "Oh, yes," he stammered, "much handsomer, excuse me, I only meant . . ."

"Whatever you meant is all one to me," the butterfly

replied. He arched his thin body affectedly and played with his delicate feelers.

Bambi looked at him, enchanted. "How elegant you are!" he said. "How elegant and fine! And how splendid and white your wings are!"

The butterfly spread his wings wide apart, then raised them till they folded together like an upright sail.

"Oh," cried Bambi, "I know that you are handsomer than the flowers. Besides, you can fly and the flowers can't because they grow on stems, that's why."

The butterfly spread his wings. "It's enough," he said, "that I can fly." He soared so lightly that Bambi could hardly see him or follow his flight. His wings moved gently and gracefully. Then he fluttered into the sunny air.

"I only sat still that long on your account," he said, balancing in the air in front of Bambi. "Now I'm going."

That was how Bambi found the meadow.

A TREE CALLED MOSES

Laura Nelson Baker

The tree called Moses grows on the side of a 9,000-foot-mountain in California, near Sequoia National Forest. The peak of the mountain was named Moses about a hundred years ago by a government surveyor. Later, the men of the forest service began to call it the Moses tree, after the mountain peak.

The Moses tree is very old. When Jesus of Nazareth was born in Bethlehem, the tree had already lived through more than five hundred birthdays. When Christopher Columbus reached America in 1492, the Moses tree was at least 2,000 years old.

The Moses tree is a giant sequoia. To most people, trees like Moses are known as "Big Trees," or the Sierra redwood.

The Big Trees grow in only one place in the world, in central California, from Placer County south to Tulare County. There on the western slopes of the Sierra Nevada mountains, in a strip about 250 miles in length, there are about seventy-five groves, growing at elevations from 3,500 to 8,500 feet. The largest contains many thousands of trees, the smallest only six. These giant trees are the last survivors of what was once a widespread race of trees in the

Northern Hemisphere. Only in this one small area is the climate and environment still right for the propagation of the Big Trees.

One autumn day, on the side of a large mountain, a squirrel with a long tail ran swiftly up the ridged bark of a tall, cinnamon-colored tree. The day was warm, and the air hummed with the sounds of millions of insects and the cries and calls of hundreds of birds.

Up at the top of the tree—a giant sequoia—a slight breeze stirred the scale-like leaves or needles. A few of the needles drifted to the ground. The squirrel, undisturbed by the falling needles, stopped his climb at a place where the tree's branches stretched out from the trunk. The little animal seemed to be deciding which way to go. After a brief pause, he ran out onto one of the branches to a place where many small seedcones hung. The squirrel, reddish in color like the sequoia itself, used its teeth to cut several cones the size of a small egg from the tree branch. The light green cones fell onto a thick bed of duff, duff being a mixture of fallen needles, old leaves, cones, bits of wood and other decayed and decaying matter. When the squirrel had a good harvest waiting for him on the ground he whistled, sounding more like a bird than a squirrel, and ran back down the tree, chattering noisily. He sat beside his pile of cones and began to tear seeds no bigger than flakes of rolled oats from under the scales of the cones and to eat them.

From a nearby pine tree, a blue jay scolded the squirrel for a few minutes and then flew away. A chipmunk whose home was in a hole in the pine tree crept around the trunk and peered down at the squirrel and his store of cones, but apparently decided to hunt his own food instead of waiting for the squirrel to abandon his treasure.

After a few more minutes, a second squirrel joined the first. The second squirrel also began to break off the scales of the cones and eat the sequoia seeds.

Finally the stomachs of both animals were full. But winter was not far away. The squirrels sensed this from the shortening days, the crispness of the nights on the mountain, and the drying grasses in a mountain meadow nearby. So they broke apart the remaining cones in the pile and raced off with the seeds they had harvested. They carried them to a hiding place that the first squirrel had discovered a few days earlier. The hiding place was between two large roots of a fir tree. The squirrel had dug down through the fallen needles of the fir into the soil below and made a storage cupboard for his winter's supply of food. In this cupboard the two squirrels now put the seeds they had removed from the sequoia cones and covered the spot over with loose soil and dead leaves. Both animals then went racing off toward a pine tree with red bark in large squares, like patches. This was a different pine tree from the one in which the chipmunk lived. On this pine, large cones gleamed in the light of the sun and invited the sharp-toothed harvesters to further adventures.

Later that day, the slight wind that had sent scale-like needles drifting to the ground while the squirrel was climbing the sequoia's trunk, grew stronger. The wind shook the tree's branches enough to loosen more cones and send them tumbling to the duff below, but because the duff contained no mineral soil, the seeds in the wind-tumbled cones would have no chance to grow. They would decay and become part of the duff bed itself.

When snow came to Moses Mountain that year it covered the squirrels' hiding place with white. The hole at the base of the fir tree was only one of many hiding places that the pair had made use of, and they may have forgotten about the hole or thought the snow too deep for them to trouble about the cones they had so carefully buried. They did not come back to the fir tree that winter.

Deep snows weight the branches of all the evergreens in the mountains during the winter, covering their greens and blue-greens with white. On nights when there is little wind, millions of stars strike sparks of light from the clean, fresh snow, but on stormy nights the great boughs of the fir, the pine, and the sequoia toss some of their snow frosting to the ground.

The ground underneath the fir tree was protected from the sharp cold by its covering of dead leaves and on top of that by the snow. In the squirrel cupboard, the sequoia cones with their many seeds, each one in a thin, protective case, lay buried in the good, nourishing soil and waited for spring and warmth.

Spring comes late in the high Sierra, and the snow stays long under the firs and pines and cedars. In May, however, when the small greenish-yellow blossoms of the dogwood tree and their large white and pinkish scales set the lower mountainsides ablaze with soft beauty, the deep snow beneath the fir tree slowly melted. Moisture seeped down to the sequoia cones in their hiding place, freeing the seeds and, working with the soil, dissolving part of the case around the seeds.

Now at last the seeds could begin to grow. Some of them, however, were not fertile. Their centers, which in healthy, life-giving seeds are white, were brown. The brown-centered seeds would later decay, becoming part of the earth under the fir tree.

But, many of the seeds under the fir tree were good seeds, and these began to swell with the first warmth of the spring sun. The Moses seed was a good seed. It began early to push its way out of the ground, sending ahead of itself a tiny part of its rust-colored case as a shield against possible dangers above ground.

Some of the other seeds that had been carried by the squirrels to the hiding place at the base of the fir tree were as healthy as the Moses seed. Several of them also began to push upward.

The fir tree under which the

seeds were starting to grow was very tall and its branches, high above the ground, let sunlight fall between them onto the barely visible plants, so that soon the spiny leaves began to unfold.

Other living things were also growing on the mountainside and in the nearby meadow and the valley far below. A long-tailed mouse, streaked with light brown along the sides of his body, sprang from a hiding place beneath a red-branched bush one morning and landed beside the Moses seedling. The mouse stood for almost a minute, his small ears alert, his round eyes wide, in the slight shade of the little Moses tree, and then with another shove of his strong hind legs, took off into the underbrush.

On the edge of a mountain stream in the same part of the mountain forest, a gray bird perched on a rock. He sent his bright flute music out over the water as though celebrating something before he began to dip and skim above the stream with small, chattering cries. The water ouzel disappeared under a rocky plateau at the edge of the stream. In a nest of moss under the rock's jutting edge, four white eggs were being kept warm by the bird's mate.

And in the mountain meadow, deer munched the wild grass and plants. The young fawns sometimes broke away from their mothers, the does, to hunt out some new and perhaps more exciting food. Occasionally the fawns bit a leaf from a shrub or tree but spit it out again without chewing or swallowing it. They were discovering what their parents had known for a long time, that some mountain plants are not proper food for deer.

By the end of the first growing season, Moses and the other healthy sequoia seedlings were covered with sharp, narrow-tipped leaves. On the main stem these leaves all pointed toward the top of the tree. On the branches the leaves pointed toward the ends of the branches. The leaves covered the seedlings so well that each seedling looked like an oversized leaf itself— the division between a branch and its leafy twigs could hardly be seen.

The young sequoias were also growing downward. Below the surface of the earth a main root was forming. From the main root, other roots as thin as hairs spread out sidewise in several directions, to establish a foundation for the years to come when they would have to support a huge trunk and many heavy branches.

When the heavy winter snows fell on the Moses tree that first year of its life, it was almost two inches tall.

By May the Moses tree was one year old and its main stem or trunk was about a quarter of an inch thick. The young tree had a long,

long fight ahead before it could become a mature Big Tree.

Summer came and went, bringing the sunshine the Moses tree needed for growth. Winter, too, with its sheltering snows and springtime, with the snows melting into needed moisture that pushed Moses ahead. At two years of age, the tree's stem measured only about a third of an inch across, but it had grown in height to twenty inches. It had lost many of the sharp first leaves along the lower part of the stem and now had some branches a foot long spreading out from the stem's sides. The lower branches were this long; the higher ones grew progressively shorter. The tree was becoming conical in shape, a tiny undecorated Christmas tree.

In the sequoia world, a tree ten years old is still an infant tree, but like other infants, trees change as they grow. Each year the trunk of the Moses tree grew steadily, if slowly, thicker. At ten years, the trunk was about two inches across and nearly six and a half inches around. As the tree passed its fifteenth, its twentieth, its thirtieth and fortieth birthdays, its roots spread outward from the central, or tap, root to form a network under the ground that helped keep the tree from toppling in storms. The spring Moses reached the age of fifty years, it had grown to be thirty feet tall and about four feet around at the base of the main trunk.

Storms on a high mountain often bring winds strong enough to uproot weak, young, or diseased trees. When it stormed, the feathery tops of the pines and firs in the Moses forest became giant green brooms that seemed to sweep the wind ahead of them, although it was actually the wind that swept the trees.

In spring the wind brought rain pounding down on the trees and on the creatures that lived in or under or near them. In winter, it brought snow. When the snow was unusually heavy on the branches of the older trees, the branches broke and came crashing down. One such heavy limb fell against the Moses tree on its way to the ground. The young sequoia, not yet sixty years old, rocked sidewise from the force of the falling limb, but straightened again as the dead bough slid off its graceful branches. The sequoia's trunk and branches were still flexible, able to bend with the wind and avoid being broken.

The fir tree at whose base the Moses seed had first been buried by the squirrel was not as fortunate as the young sequoia. At the height of one great storm it began to tremble on its base, a base which had been shaken many times before by strong winds, until it no longer held firm. Sometime in the middle of the night, when the storm had begun to die, the gray barked tree that had lived perhaps 150 years, crashed to the floor of the forest, crushing many shrubs and smaller trees under it as it fell.

The tree, a white fir, fell in the opposite direction from the Moses tree. Although the ground under the Moses tree trembled from the impact of the fallen fir, the sequoia stayed firmly rooted.

The death of the white fir, like the destruction of the other seedling sequoias near Moses, meant that once again it had been given a better chance to grow. For now more sunlight came through the forest and there was more space for roots. When springtime arrived, the tree was able to stretch its branches upward more easily.

By the time Moses had become a hundred years old most of the lower branches along its trunk had either fallen or been broken off. Its crown was a feathery mass of green, with here and there along the main stem a bright green ornament of new, fresh growth. Bark had formed in thin flakes, the flakes piling on top of each other to create the thick bark evident in fully grown trees. Underneath the purplish-brown outer covering of the bark were many fibers or hairs. These fibers were brown, too, but a different, lighter brown, the color of cinnamon.

As the Moses tree's trunk grew thicker, the bark sometimes split, leaving the sapwood, which is the wood closest to the outer edge of a tree, uncovered. The sapwood on the Moses tree did not stay

uncovered very long. The healthy sequoia grew new bark over the exposed places. This constant renewing of bark made the Moses tree, as it grew older, develop a fluted bark all along its trunk.

Other changes were taking place in the Moses tree. At the base of the trunk, a red-brown liquid, or sap, developed while Moses was still a young sequoia. As the tree grew taller and thicker, this sap spread upward. And when Moses was nearly old enough to produce flowers and cones, the red sap spread through the tree's branches, helping to protect the entire tree from insects and fire.

At the age of 150 years, Moses was a hundred feet tall. Although some sequoias become seed trees by the time they are 150, the Moses tree was not yet ready to flower and bear cones like those that had hung on the parent tree before the pine squirrels had cut the cones off for food.

It was very silent in the forest where Moses stood on a late spring day in the year the tree was 200 years old. By then it was 140 feet tall and measured close to ten feet around its trunk. For many months snow had piled up beneath the pines and firs and other sequoias growing on the side of Moses Mountain. The snow lay like a shawl on the larger tree branches.

As the sun climbed higher in the sky, however, the snow warmed and began to fall from the branches, making soft sounds to break the forest silence of winter.

For the Moses tree, that spring was unlike other springs it had known. While snow still covered the ground below it, the top of the tree put forth flowers for the first time. The blooms were the color of butter and about the size of a tiny bee. They covered the crown of the Moses tree, turning it into a huge yellow flower. Bumblebees came out of their nests in the ground to feed on the sequoia blossoms' nectar.

Moses now had only a few tiny branches along the lower part of its trunk but at the top, far above the ground, great arms spread outward, waving green leaves in the winds. The yellow flowers lasted only a short time because the winds shook the petals and pollen down onto the forest floor. But the flowers were soon replaced by the first cones of the many that the tree would bear. One cone was kicked loose from the tree by the feet of a chipmunk racing along a branch. The cone fell to the ground and rolled to a stop beside a pine cone that had lain under the snow all winter. The pine cone, dark brown against the clear, bright green of the sequoia, was almost ten times as long, even though the sugar pine from which it had fallen was much younger and smaller than the Moses tree.

For other creatures in the forest, the first cones of the Moses tree mattered little. For them the pattern of days and seasons went on as it always had.

A huge bear came along the creek that cut across the mountainside a quarter of a mile from the Big Trees. The bear, a grizzly, stopped at a place where the snow on the creek had melted. He stood up on his hind legs and looked around him, his white-tipped fur looking like the snow blanket on the bank of the creek. Suddenly the bear dropped to his feet again and crouched above the water. His paw, armed with long, heavy claws, flashed into the water and came out with a fish, which he swallowed. After the bear had eaten his fill he lumbered toward the Moses tree and, stretching himself to his full height, he scraped his paws down its length. Then he dropped down on all fours again and disappeared in the direction of his cave in the rocks west of the Moses tree.

Other living things also began to stir in the forest world. Violet plants, which had been hiding under the snow, thrust heart-shaped leaves out from the soil as soon as the snow blanket melted. As spring moved toward summer, the violets opened their small blue petals and gave their own special fragrance to the mountain air. So also did the orange wallflowers. And wild buckwheat was sprouting on the barer parts of the hillsides across from the Moses tree.

As spring moved on into summer, and all of the snow melted from under the forest trees, birds, which had been scarce during the winter months, returned. A hummingbird very little larger than the green sequoia cone, perched on a dead twig near the Moses tree. Like a brilliant lavender flower moved by a breeze, he turned his head from side to side and then began to make deep, narrow U swings in the air. Below, concealed in the new leaves of a red-limbed manzanita bush, sat a female bird. When the bright-colored male bird had made his excited swings back and forth in the air, he suddenly flew upward into the top branches of the Moses tree. Resting his whirring wings for only an instant, he shot swiftly downward toward

the female, ending his flight with a soft courting cry.

Later the hummingbirds built a nest on a twig under a large branch of a pine tree, and the mother laid two tiny white eggs in the nest.

Above Moses' crown, in the high sunshine, an eagle sometimes circled and soared, the light turning his brown feathers to gold. But the golden eagle did not come down into the forest to build his nest. When he had found his mate, the two huge birds made a large home out of sticks, high on a rocky cliff.

A bird on the Moses Mountain that had not waited for summer before singing his shining songs was the water ouzel. All winter long the ouzel sang and when spring came, he kept up the same melody. When the water in the stream where the ouzel and his mate yearly built their nest was free of ice and snow, the birds dipped often into the creek, diving under the surface. Because of their water loving antics, the ouzels are sometimes called dipper birds.

The ouzel that sang the year that Moses first produced flowers and cones was, of course, not the same ouzel that had been singing and nesting at the time the Moses tree had been only a seed. Generations of such singers had been born, lived, and died during the time that Moses had been growing. Generations of animals, too, had followed each other, giving birth to babies of their own kind, babies that grew up, found mates and had more babies of their own.

There were no animals or birds or flowers in the forest as old as Moses; but there were trees, when the Moses tree was 200 years old, that were much older. About 300 feet away, nearer the fork of the river, other large sequoias, old when Moses was born, towered over the younger members of the sequoia family. And there were fir trees on the mountainside that were 300 years old. One sugar pine was over 400 and many others were as old as Moses. Beside the older sugar pines and firs, the Moses tree was still young.

Moses was, however, now tall enough to share the Sierra sunshine with the other large trees. In summer, that sunlight hit the treetops then fell in ribbons across the forest floor, turning the red flowers of the columbine into brilliant trumpets.

Summers were sunshine, sudden storms, lightning—an ever threatening danger for the forest— life, activity, and growth. Then in late summer or early fall, when the sudden summer storms were over, a more steady rain would begin. It dropped in straight, wet needles down through the trees, soaking the underbrush and the duff and the leaves of the giant sequoias. After a day or more of this kind of rain, fog would build up on the mountaintop, rising like steam from the ground. It would fill the branches of the Moses tree and the other trees on Moses Mountain, hiding their tops in a wet, thick fog-cloud.

Later, when the weather was colder, this rain would be snow. Then many of the birds who had nested in the trees and shrubs would leave until it was time for warmth to come again to the air. The bears retreated into rock dens and only a few birds stayed around to sing or chirp.

Some mountain creatures did not hide. The hares that all summer long wore brown coats to match the trunks of the trees and the dry, fallen pine and fir needles, changed their brown coats for white ones when winter came.

A wind began to rise, stirring the leaves of the sequoias, pines and firs. The stars were soon covered over with dark clouds and the wind increased. A new storm was on its way to Moses Mountain. The wind blew ferociously against the Moses tree, making its crown shake and dance as it waited for the snow. Some of its first crop of cones fell to the ground but most of them stayed on the tree. It would take two years for the cones to become ripe enough to produce seed that might sometime become new sequoia trees.

excerpt from

Hands Up!

Ruth Goode

Only People Have Hands

Look around and you will see that most animals do not
have hands. Birds have wings where their hands would be.
Fish have fins. Most animals have four feet and they walk
on all fours.

Cows and horses, goats and deer have hoofs. So do
giraffes.

These are animals that live on plant foods. They eat
grass and leaves, and the twigs and bark of trees. Animals
with hoofs run and walk on the tips of their toes. A hoof
is a special kind of toenail that grows very hard and tough.
It grows big enough to cover the ends of the toes
altogether, like a hard little shoe. Their hoofs help these
animals to run fast over rough ground, to get away from
the animals that hunt them.

Hunting animals have paws that go softly over the
ground, almost without a sound. Their quiet paws are very
useful in hunting. Cats and lions, dogs and wolves are
hunting animals. Members of the cat family have toenails
that are claws. They have special muscles in their paws to
push their claws out for fighting or climbing.

Seals and whales have flippers that work like paddles
when they swim. When you learn to swim, your
swimming teacher tells you to keep your fingers together,
so that they will work like a seal's flippers in the water.

On monkeys, all four feet are very much like hands, thumbs and all—very useful for swinging through the trees and picking the fruit that they eat. When they run on the ground they go on all four feet.

Some of the big apes—the chimpanzees and gorillas—walk on their two hind feet and the knuckles of their hands. Watch them do this, the next time you go to the zoo.

Look at all the animals, and you will see that only people have hands that are never used as feet, except to do acrobatic tricks. Only people have hands that they use just to hold and carry things and work with tools.

Our hands make us different from all other living creatures.

How Do the Animals Manage without Hands?

If the animals have no hands like ours, how do they do all the things they do?

They all have different ways.

Your dog holds down his bone with his paw while he chews at it. Your cat wets her forepaw with her tongue to wash her face, and then she washes herself everywhere else with her tongue. A mother cat washes her kittens all over with her tongue, until they learn to wash themselves.

Birds pick up things with their beaks. They carry straws and whatever they need up into the tree to make a nest, and they weave the nest with their beaks.

Birds that eat seeds crack the seeds in their beaks and spit out the shells. You can watch the house finches do that at your bird feeder.

The weaver finch holds a thorn in its beak the way you would hold a tool in your hand, and it uses the thorn the same way. It pokes out grubs and insects from the bark of a tree for its food.

A sea gull drops a clam on the rocks and then swoops down to peck the juicy clam out of its broken shell.

A California sea otter has an even trickier way of getting a shellfish out of its shell. The otter floats on its back with a flat stone on its chest and bangs the shellfish on the rock with its two forepaws until the shell breaks.

A squirrel sits up and cracks a nut with its strong teeth, holding the nut between its two forepaws.

A monkey can hold a banana in one hand. It is almost the only animal that can do that. But it could probably hold the banana just as well with its foot!

Monkeys can pick bugs and burrs out of their own and each other's coats with their fingertips. So can some apes. The baboons are apes that eat seeds, and they can pick up things as tiny as we can.

A chimpanzee is a very clever ape, but it can never pick up small objects with a thumb and forefinger. It has a long palm and a short thumb, too short to put thumb tip and fingertip together. If you gave a chimpanzee a grape, it would take the grape and hold it with its thumb against the side of its palm.

But if you gave a chimpanzee a piece of string you would never be able to take the string back, unless the chimpanzee wanted to give it to you. It would hold the string with its thumb against its palm, then fold its palm over that, and then curl its long fingers over that, making a fist with the thumb inside. The chimpanzee's double-lock grip is special for the way it gets its food. It can swing out on a thin branch or jungle vine and hang there by one hand without slipping, while it reaches for the young, tender leaves at the end of the branch.

excerpt from

GORILLA GORILLA

Carol Fenner
illustrations by Symeon Shimin

This selection is taken from the book Gorilla Gorilla, *which tells the story of a gorilla captured in the wild and placed in a zoo. Even though this particular gorilla is fictional, the book tells a realistic story of how gorillas behave in the wild and in captivity.*

He was born, wet and tiny
and gray,
one wet and gray morning
when the mists lay heavy in the rain forest.
His mother carried him close
in her big arms,
warm in her glossy hair.
His mouth was open a lot.
His appetite was endless.

Before many months
he could ride on his mother's back,
clutching
the hairs on her shoulders
while she moved about with the others,
feeding among the wild celery and thistles
or in the places of bamboo.

He grew.
His hair became long,
covering his body.
He learned which leafy greens
were tasty
and where to find the tender parts of bamboo
and wild celery.

Every evening he watched his mother
pull young tree shoots
and leafy bushes toward her,
bend and trample them
with her powerful feet
to make their nest for the night.

She arranged smaller leaves
and bushes about her,
and when she settled down
her great weight pressed the springy branches
into a mattress beneath her.

242

Soon he could make his own nest—
sometimes in a tree,
bending the leafy branches under him—
sometimes on the ground.
But he always left his little nest
to crawl in
beside his big warm mother
and sleep nestled under her arm
or against her round, rumbling belly.

He grew.
Sometimes during the day
he rode on his mother
while the group roamed
through the wet, dense forest
or fragrant meadows,
feeding.

But other times
he walked by himself on the ground,
pulling up his own food,
staying near his mother.
He looked for the prickly thistle
and ate it—
flowers, leaves, prickles
and all. He looked for
nettles and blackberries
and their leaves,
sweet herbs, bedstraw,
and the tender insides of wild celery.
He tried everything.
What he didn't like he spat out.

He grew.
He watched the bigger young ones
wrestle.
When he was a year old
he began to play with them,
to wrestle and roll and
follow the leader.

He was no longer the smallest
in the group.
Now there were new ones,
littler ones,
watching him.
He liked to climb and swing from vines,
to somersault,
to slap his chest
and kick his legs,
to walk across his mother's belly.

Day followed day.
Mist in the morning.
Sometimes rain
sliding off his back as he huddled
with the others.
Sometimes sun
warming their dozing bodies,
gleaming in their blue-black hair.

They kept moving always.
They followed the wild celery
and berry bush, followed
the silvery back of their huge leader
with his great arms
and stiff, crested crown.

The young one grew and grew.
By the time he was three
he was sleeping in his own nest
most of the time.
There were moments
during the browsing
drowsy days
when he felt a tickling excitement.
Then he would toss up leaves and branches
into the air
with quick and furious energy
like the older males.
He began to watch the silver-backed leader
more closely.

One afternoon
when the drops of a brief rain
were still on the leaves,
he noticed a sound,
a soft repeated hoot.
He had heard it before
but it had always been an unimportant noise
like vague and distant thunder.
Now he listened with a new curiosity.
The hoots grew louder and more rapid,
filling him with excitement.

248

He stopped chewing. He dropped a leafy stalk
he had pulled up
and followed the sound. The swift hoot-hoot
seemed strange to him
in his fascination
yet, at the same time, it was familiar
like the other sounds of the forest.
It came from the clearing where the group rested.
The females and youngsters had pulled into a cluster
at one end. The grown males
paced at the edge near the trees.

In the center of the clearing
sat the great silver-backed one,
his head thrown back,
his lips shaped around the beat
of the sound.
The young one did not join the others
but climbed for a better view
into an overhanging tree.
The air trembled with the silverback's swift hooting.
The great leader reached out
with a light swing
and plucked a leaf from a nearby bush.
He placed it like a flower
between his long, flat lips
and continued to hoot.

The hoots grew louder and faster,
faster and faster still.
Suddenly the huge leader
thrust himself to his short legs.
He tore up great clumps of bush and vine,
tossed them with a furious heave
high into the air,
and began to thump his massive chest
like a frenzied drummer.
The drumming boomed and leapt
into the leafy jungle,
across the high meadows
and jutting cliffs of the rain forest—
an increasing chorus of beats.
The hoots melted
into a blurred growl.

In the meadow
a black buffalo raised his head,
listening.
Birds flew up protesting.
As far as a mile away
a little red forest duiker
bounded nervously into the brush;
a leopard paused in his stalking,
nostrils to the wind.

The young one watched,
the half-chewed food forgotten in his mouth.

Suddenly
the great silverback dropped to all fours
and ran furiously sideways
thrashing his arms and ripping at the ground.
A youngster
who had strayed into the leader's path
was knocked off its feet.
A wild swing of his great arms,
a violent thump on the ground,
and it was over.
Quiet.
The sun shone undisturbed
through the heavy trees.

The bowled-over infant stood up,
shook its head,
and looked around for its mother.
The young one
sat in the tree for a long time afterward,
slowly chewing,
his excitement melting
into the drowsy afternoon.

He was to witness the great silverback's display
with increasing fascination
many times after that.
When the group had been disturbed
by the odor of men
or other groups like themselves
or some excitement he was too young
to recognize,
he came to expect
the leader's violent and compelling ritual.
He began to imitate the lordly crouch,
the great roar.
He even tried the whole kingly ritual himself,
learning to thump the hollow song
from his own expanding chest.
Sometimes
after the mists
had risen and left the forest,
he felt great happiness
in his body.
Then he, too, would thump his chest and toss
great clumps of leaves
high and joyfully into the air.

Day followed misty day
with rains and occasional sunshine.
His hair grew long, blue-black,
and glossy.
He could swing his long arms
and lift himself at a run
into the trees.

He often slept in the trees now,
his nest roughly woven of bent-in branches,
that rested in the crotch of the tree.
His brow had grown jutting
and fierce,
but his eyes were still soft
and brown
like his mother's,
like all their eyes.

When he was eight years old
he was almost full grown.
He was big for his age
and very handsome.
The young females
slapped at him playfully.
Young males avoided him.
On his crown
grew the beginnings
of a stiff, tufted crest
like that of the silver-backed leader.
His body had taken on the heavy muscles
of the young male.
The great silverback began to notice him
with cautious interest,
sensing in the younger
the stirrings of a future lord.

He weighed close to 300 pounds.
He was strong and glossy
and magnificent.

When the hunters came
into the eastern Congo
they were looking for magnificent animals.
They wanted healthy specimens,
young ones.
They wanted the best.
They came from another continent
across the seas.
They wore many clothes
and carried loud weapons.
They hired local trackers,
men from the villages,
to help them catch the wild animals
of Africa
for the people of another continent
to look at, and marvel.

They caught the leopard
and the lion in the bush of the lowlands.
They took the giraffe
from the high grass range,
the hippopotamus from the river bed
and the elephant who had come there to drink at dusk.
And they came into the rain forests
of the highlands,
looking for the mountain gorilla.

It had been an uneasy day,
a close, heavy day
that waited for rain.
The great silverback had led his group
deep among the trees for the night.
They built their nests
with slow, heavy movements
and dropped to sleep.
The young one felt lonely
and disturbed that evening.
He built his nest on the ground
to be closer to the others.

He was awakened abruptly,
jolted from deep in his sleep
by the blood-tingling scream
of the great silverback.
At the same time
he felt the faint slap
of something dense,
yet light,
fall down about him.
Rain?
A web of frozen air?
A net!

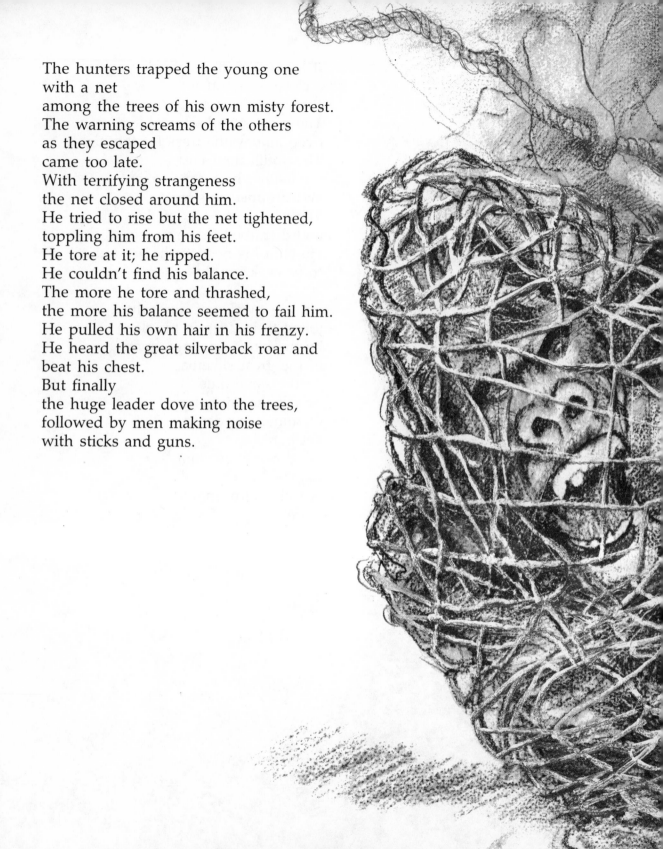

The hunters trapped the young one
with a net
among the trees of his own misty forest.
The warning screams of the others
as they escaped
came too late.
With terrifying strangeness
the net closed around him.
He tried to rise but the net tightened,
toppling him from his feet.
He tore at it; he ripped.
He couldn't find his balance.
The more he tore and thrashed,
the more his balance seemed to fail him.
He pulled his own hair in his frenzy.
He heard the great silverback roar and
beat his chest.
But finally
the huge leader dove into the trees,
followed by men making noise
with sticks and guns.

He felt himself lifted,
swaying dizzily. His stomach heaved—
his weight no longer belonged to him.
He struggled blindly in the net.
Then his body touched the floor of a truck.
He was in a cage. Bits of his broken nest
still clung to his hair.
He pounded his big chest
in fury and fear; he grasped
the bars of the cage
and shook them in his powerful hands.
The enemy net was still caught across his shoulders.
"He's a beauty," said one hunter to the other.
And they drove him away
while he raged with the tangled net
in the back of their truck.
From somewhere
deep in the forest
the silverback screamed his warning
over and over.

After a day of sickening travel in the truck,
he was loaded aboard a transport jet
and taken across the ocean
to another continent.
The motion of the plane
made him listless and ill.
He lay on his back
with his legs sprawled
and his soft eyes fixed on the ceiling.
He did not move
except to roll his eyes
toward the man who brought his food.
He did not eat.

All around him was the close smell
of other animals.
Sometimes the tight, helpless growl
of the panther in the next cage
made his sprawled legs twitch.
But he did not move from his back.
When the jet landed,
the big ape's cage
was lowered from the hold
into another truck.
The unfamiliar smells and sounds
of this strange place
made him roll up to his feet.
He clutched the bars of his cage
and peered from under his fierce brow
at the new shapes of things,
at the pale, choppy faces of people.
He was bewildered and sore in his heart.

They took him
to a large zoo.
He was put into an indoor cage
with an outdoor yard
surrounded by high walls and a moat.
There was a tall tree in the yard.
The moat was full of water.
They put a sign
in front of his walled yard.
It said, "Gorilla gorilla beringei,"
and underneath it said,
"Habitat: East Africa."

Gorilla gorilla
did not go outside
into his walled yard.
He lay on his back
in his cage
on the cement floor
with his legs sprawled,
his soft eyes fixed on the ceiling.
He did not eat.

Next to his cage
was a shaggy red orang-utan
who liked apples.
On the other side
were three baboons
who quarreled among themselves
and showed off
for the people
who looked into their cage.

Gorilla gorilla lay on his back
in the indoor cage.
He did not eat.
He stared at the ceiling.

One day
the long, shaggy arm
of the orang-utan
reached through the bars
for Gorilla gorilla's uneaten apples.
Gorilla gorilla turned his fierce brow
toward the orang-utan.
His eyes were angry.
Immediately he rolled to his feet
and slapped the shaggy red arm away.
Orang-utan leapt back with a scream.
Then Gorilla gorilla ate.
He devoured his food.
Later he sat in a corner of his cage
glaring at Orang-utan.

After that he always ate his food.
And sometimes
he went outside into his walled yard
to lie on his back
by the single tree
with his legs sprawled,
staring at the sky.
His hair
began to grow glossy again.

In the afternoons
when school children came to the zoo,
he would lift himself partway
through his door
and leave only his back end
for them to see.
This was not very interesting
to the children.
They always moved on
to the baboons,
who made them laugh with their tricks.
Or they watched Orang-utan,
who climbed about
showing off his shaggy red hair.
No one found Gorilla gorilla
magnificent.

On Sunday afternoons
the zoo was always full of people
peering into the yards and cages.
The panther paced,
restless and frustrated.

The baboons did their tricks
so they could watch the people laugh and clap.
Orang-utan
displayed his amazing shaggy grace.
Sunday was a lively day.
The people watched the animals.
The animals watched the people.
There was clapping and laughing
and the chattering of many voices.

Only Gorilla gorilla
refused to see the people.
He leaned halfway through his door.
All anyone could see of him
was his broad backside.

One day
Orang-utan next door
was moved to another cage.
It took the keepers
all morning to get him out of his old cage.
They finally tempted him out with apples.
For several days
the cage next to Gorilla gorilla
was empty.
He had just begun to miss
his shaggy red neighbor
when the keepers brought in
someone new.

The new one
was another gorilla,
a young female.

excerpt from

Lassie Come–Home

Eric Knight

"I Never Want Another Dog"

The dog was not there! That was all Joe Carraclough knew. That day he had come out of school with the others, and had gone racing across the yard in a rush of gladness that you see at all schools, all the world over, when lessons are over for the day. Almost automatically, by a habit ingrained through hundreds of days, he had gone to the gate where Lassie always waited. And she was not there!

Joe Carraclough stood, a sturdy, pleasant-faced boy, trying to reason it out. The broad forehead over his brown eyes became wrinkled. At first, he found himself unable to realize that what his senses told him could be true.

He looked up and down the street. Perhaps Lassie was late! He knew that could not be the reason, though, for animals are not like human beings. Human beings have watches and clocks, and yet they are always finding themselves "five minutes behind time." Animals need no machines to tell time. There is something inside them that is more accurate than clocks. It is a "time sense," and it never fails them. They know, surely and truly, exactly when it is time to take part in some well-established routine of life.

Joe Carraclough knew that. He had often talked it over with his father, asking him how it was that Lassie knew when it was time to start for the school gate. Lassie could not be late.

Joe Carraclough stood in the early summer sunshine, thinking of this. Suddenly a flash came into his mind.

Perhaps she had been run over!

Even as this thought brought panic to him, he was dismissing it. Lassie was far too well trained to wander carelessly in the streets. She always moved daintily and surely along the pavements of the village. Then, too, there was very little traffic of any kind in Greenall Bridge. The main motor road went along the valley by the river a mile away. Only a small road came up to the village, and that became merely narrow footpaths father along when it reached the flat moorland.

Perhaps someone had stolen Lassie!

Yet this could hardly be true. No stranger could so much as put a hand on Lassie unless one of the Carracloughs was there to order her to submit to it. And, moreover, she was far too well known for miles around Greenall Bridge for anyone to dare to steal her.

But where could she be?

Joe Carraclough solved his problem as hundreds of thousands of boys solve their problems the world over. He ran home to tell his mother.

Down the main street he went, racing as fast as he could. Without pausing, he went past the shops on High Street, through the village to the little lane going up the hillside, up the lane and through a gate, along a garden path, and then through the cottage door, to cry out:

"Mother? Mother—something's happened to Lassie! She didn't meet me!"

As soon as he had said it, Joe Carraclough knew that there was something wrong. No one in the cottage jumped up and asked him what the matter was. No one seemed afraid that something dire had happened to their fine dog.

Joe noticed that. He stood with his back to the door, waiting. His mother stood with her eyes lowered toward the table where she was setting out the tea-time meal. For a second she was still. Then she looked at her husband.

Joe's father was sitting on a low stool before the fire, his head turned toward his son. Slowly, without speaking, he turned back to the fire and stared into it intently.

"What is it, Mother?" Joe cried suddenly. "What's wrong?"

Mrs. Carraclough set a plate on the table slowly and then she spoke.

"Well, somebody's got to tell him," she said, as if to the air.

Her husband made no move. She turned her head toward her son.

"Ye might as well know it right off, Joe," she said. "Lassie won't be waiting at school for ye no more. And there's no use crying about it."

"Why not? What's happened to her?"

Mrs. Carraclough went to the fireplace and set the kettle over it. She spoke without turning.

"Because she's sold. That's why not."

"Sold!" the boy echoed, his voice high. "Sold! What did ye sell her for—Lassie—what did ye sell her for?"

His mother turned angrily.

"Now she's sold, and gone, and done with. So don't ask any more questions. They won't change it. She's gone, so that's that—and let's say no more about it."

"But Mother . . ."

The boy's cry rang out, high and puzzled. His mother interrupted him.

"Now no more! Come and have your tea! Come on. Sit ye down!"

Obediently the boy went to his place at the table. The woman turned to the man at the fireplace.

"Come on, Sam, and eat. Though Lord knows, it's poor enough stuff to set out for tea . . ."

The woman grew quiet as her husband rose with an angry suddenness. Then, without speaking a word, he strode to the door, took his cap from a peg, and went out. The door slammed behind him. For a moment after, the cottage was silent. Then the woman's voice rose, scolding in tone.

"Now, see what ye've done! Got thy father all angry. I suppose ye're happy now."

Wearily she sat in her chair and stared at the table. For a long time the cottage was silent. Joe knew it was unfair of his mother to blame him for what was happening. Yet he knew, too, that it was his mother's way of covering up her own hurt. It was exactly the same as her scolding. That was the way with the people in those parts. They were rough, stubborn people, used to living a rough, hard life. When anything happened that touched their emotions, they covered up their feelings. The women scolded and chattered to hide their hurts. They did not mean anything by it. After it was over . . .

"Come on, Joe. Eat up!"

His mother's voice was soft and patient now.

The boy stared at his plate, unmoving.

"Come on, Joe. Eat your bread and butter. Look—nice new bread, I just baked today. Don't ye want it?"

The boy bent his head lower.

"I don't want any," he said in a whisper.

"Oh, dogs, dogs, dogs," his mother flared. Her voice rose in anger again. "All this trouble over one dog. Well, if ye ask me, I'm glad Lassie's gone. That I am. As much trouble to take care of as a child! Now she's gone, and it's done with, and I'm glad—I am. I'm glad!"

Mrs. Carraclough shook her plump self and sniffed. Then she took her handkerchief from her apron pocket and blew her nose. Finally she looked at her son, still sitting, unmoving. She shook her head sadly and spoke. Again her voice was patient and kind.

"Joe, come here," she said.

The boy rose and stood by his mother. She put her plump arm around him and spoke, her head turned to the fire.

"Look Joe, ye're getting to be a big lad now, and ye can understand. Ye see—well, ye know things aren't going so well for us these days. Ye know how it is. And we've got to have food on the table, and we've got to pay our rent—and Lassie was worth a lot of money and—well, we couldn't afford to keep her, that's all. Now these are poor times and ye mustn't—ye mustn't upset thy father. He's worrying enough as it is—and—well, that's all. She's gone."

Young Joe Carraclough stood by his mother in the cottage. He did understand. Even a boy of twelve years in Greenall Bridge knew what "poor times" were.

For years, for as long as children could remember, their fathers had worked in the Wellington Pit beyond the village. They had gone on-shift, off-shift, carrying their snap boxes of food and their colliers' lanterns; and they had worked at bringing up the rich coal. Then times had become "poor." The pit went on "slack time," and the men earned less. Sometimes the work had picked up, and the men had gone on full time.

Then everyone was glad. It did not mean luxurious living for them, for in the coal-mining villages people lived a hard life at best. But it was a life of courage and family unity, at least, and if the food that was set on the tables was plain, there was enough of it to go round.

Only a few months ago, the pit had closed down altogether. The big wheel at the top of the shaft spun no more. The men no longer flowed in a stream to the pit-yard at the shift changes. Instead, they signed on at the Labor Exchange. They stood on the corner by the Exchange, waiting for work. But no work came. It seemed that they were in what the newspapers called "the stricken areas"—sections of the country from which all industry had gone. Whole villages of people were out of work. There was no way of earning a living. The Government gave the people a "dole"—a weekly sum of money—so that they could stay alive.

Joe knew this. He had heard people talking in the village. He had seen the men at the Labor Exchange. He knew that his father no longer went to work. He knew, too, that his father and mother never spoke of it before him—that in their rough, kind way they had tried to keep their burdens of living from bearing also on his young shoulders.

Though his brain told him these things, his heart still cried for Lassie. But he silenced it. He stood steadily and then asked one question.

"Couldn't we buy her back some day, Mother?"

"Now, Joe, she was a very valuable dog, and she's worth too much for us. But we'll get another dog some day. Just wait. Times might pick up, and then we'll get another pup. Wouldn't ye like that?"

Joe Carraclough bent his head and shook it slowly. His voice was only a whisper.

"I don't ever want another dog. Never! I only want—Lassie!"

Swift Things are Beautiful

Elizabeth Coatsworth

Swift things are beautiful:
Swallows and deer,
And lightning that falls
Bright-veined and clear,
Rivers and meteors,
Wind in the wheat,
The strong-withered horse,
The runner's sure feet.

And slow things are beautiful:
The closing of day,
The pause of the wave
That curves downward to spray,
The ember that crumbles,
The opening flower,
And the ox that moves on
In the quiet of power.